D1170992

# WHISTLER

SYMPHONY IN WHITE No. 2 (*The Little White Girl*): *In the National Gallery, London.*

# WHISTLER

## By JAMES LAVER

MCMXXX

COSMOPOLITAN BOOK CORPORATION

NEW YORK

ND237
.W6L3

COPYRIGHT, 1930, BY JAMES LAVER
ALL RIGHTS RESERVED, PRINTED IN
THE U. S. A. BY J. J. LITTLE & IVES
COMPANY, NEW YORK

# CONTENTS

60168

# ILLUSTRATIONS

[ 7 ]

# ILLUSTRATIONS

[ 8 ]

## FOREWORD

More than a quarter of a century has elapsed since Whistler's death, and the dust of controversy has settled a little. In his lifetime, few men excited so much, and he was scarcely dead when the quarrels broke out anew. His relationship with other artists, his originality, or the lack of it, his honesty as a craftsman, his opinion of the Royal Academy, his place in the history of art were all eagerly disputed, and no unanimous conclusion was arrived at.

There are artists whose whole self is in their work. Not so Whistler. Indeed, his personality was always obscuring or distorting his achievement, and those who were offended by the one were unlikely to do justice to the other. An attempt to understand the man, to see through him (not in the hostile sense) to the work behind, is all the more necessary.

The mere number and extent of writings about Whistler, contemporary criticisms, legal proceedings, volumes of reminiscences, make it the more difficult to obtain a coherent picture, such a picture as I have endeavored, successfully or not, to build up here.

As soon as may be after a distinguished man's death, his "official biography" is given to the world. This is usually the work of friends or relatives, and is inevitably partizan. It would be absurd to expect from it a coldly critical appraisement of its subject's place in history. It is sufficient if it be reasonably honest and gives, as accurately as it can, all the facts it has been possible to ascertain. It should be regarded as material for biography, rather than as biography itself, and that is why "The Whistler Journal," published by the Pennells, is in some ways a more valuable book than the same authors' "Life of Whistler." For the former gives the facts with a minimum of comment, and the Pennells were extraordinarily assiduous in collecting facts (for which the world should be grateful to them) while some of their comments were singularly wide of the mark. The "Life" was a pæan to "the greatest artist of the nineteenth century," which Whistler most emphatically was not.

Yet I trust that I have resisted the temptation to write a mere counterblast to adulation, to add another example to that school of malicious biography which was recently so much in fashion. I hope I have resisted also that straining after the picturesque which converts biography into a hampered kind of fiction, inventing scenes for which there is no historical warrant by elaborating situations that, in fact, were simple enough, and spinning thought soliloquies out of the writer's own imagination.

It would have been easy to have made of Whistler's life a succession of love affairs—Fumette, Finette, Jo,

[ 10 ]

Maud, Mrs. Godwin—but the falsification would be evident. Yet it would be absurd to ignore such relationships. Women exercised a profound effect on the life and the art of Whistler; their companionship was one of the first needs of his nature, and the fact that he was not over-careful to obtain the blessing of the Church before embarking on a partnership need neither surprise nor shock us. If he threw over the Puritan principles in which he had been brought up, he did so without hypocrisy and without ostentation. That he had nothing of the Don Juan the mere length of his successive attachments is sufficient proof. Even Fumette lived with him for two years, Jo for a decade, Maud for even longer; and he was faithful to Mrs. Whistler until her death.

The time has gone when we can expect to garner many new facts. The publication of several books of reminiscences since has provided a valuable corrective to the Pennell life; but it would be unreasonable to expect any "astounding revelations" in a new biography of one who, as he himself boasted, "had no private life."

The present volume is a study of the complex and fascinating personality of a man who was also a distinguished artist. It is an attempt to present him (like one of his own pictures) bathed in the appropriate atmosphere and the proper distance inside the frame. As a personality, his background is the social life of London in the second half of the nineteenth century; as an artist his background is partly French, partly English, partly Japanese, and partly his own creation. Few artists have absorbed so many influences and remained so completely themselves. Fantin-Latour, Courbet, Rossetti, Albert Moore, Hiroshige—they all have a place, however small, in Whistler's development, and the final result is completely unlike anything they did. He is as difficult to pin down as the butterfly which he took as his symbol: a tiresome, elusive creature surprising the eye with flashes of unexpected beauty.

I would wish to make my acknowledgments to all those whose works are cited in the Bibliographical Note at the end of this volume, to those who have given me their kind permission to reproduce pictures in their possession, and to all who have helped me with criticism and advice.

J. L.

*Chelsea, 1930.*

# WHISTLER

## CHAPTER I

WHISTLER was born at Baltimore (as he informed his first biographer, Théodore Duret), at St. Petersburg (so he told the judge in the Ruskin trial), and at Lowell, Massachusetts (as the careful study of the records has at last established), on July 10, 1834. These three birthplaces may well stand for three of the most striking elements in his character: St. Petersburg for his cosmopolitanism, Baltimore for the Cavalier spirit in which all his affairs were conducted, and the despised Lowell for the inbred Puritanism from which he never managed to shake himself free. His cosmopolitanism was at once the cause of his widely extended fame and of his greatest weakness as an artist. Men are more like plants than they imagine, and artists especially suffer some obscure injury by having their roots disturbed.

If Whistler's art reached down to no rich subsoil, if it tapped no profound source of human impulse, it was because he was essentially a plant in a pot. He proved extremely successful in drawing nutriment from the air around him; he developed an exquisite bloom of a hitherto unknown variety, but his roots turned in upon themselves,

[ 15 ]

and he left no seed to propagate his kind. His art was as exquisite as a prize in a flower show, as barren as a hybrid, as shallow as cosmopolitan culture must always be.

Cosmopolitanism, however, is something that happens to a man during his lifetime; the Cavalier and Puritan elements were entwined in Whistler at birth.

America, in the twentieth century, is visibly developing its own culture, which is compounded of many elements, and in which the original English contribution will find but a small place. But a hundred years ago this was not so. The American character was still largely shaped by those who had sailed from England in the seventeenth century: the Pilgrim Fathers in the North, and the Cavalier colonists in the South.

Whistler always looked upon himself as a Southerner —hence his resentment against the chance which caused him to be born in Massachusetts—but the Puritan element in his character was none the less strongly marked. No one seems to be able ever to get rid of an ancestral Puritanism; it is the most persistent strain in nature. Conventional behavior may be abandoned; orthodox morality may be cast aside; but the Puritanism which is bred in the bone always results in the denial of the flesh in one way or another. Puritanism loses its virtue but not its force when it loses its moral impulse. What begins as a discipline ends as a desiccation, and it is not entirely fantastic to find in the dryness of Whistler's later manner, in the primness of his approach to life the ultimate results of his Puritan ancestry and upbringing.

A man's art springs from the deeper levels of his nature, and Whistler's deeper levels were Puritan. What is called a man's personality is often determined by strata less profound, although still ancestral. Whistler's attitude to the world around him was Cavalier, often extremely so; that is to say, the set of rules which governed his conduct was of the arbitrary and aristocratic kind, based on the conception of honor, rather than on that of morality. In the modern world both conceptions are obsolescent, being gradually replaced by the humanitarian notion of general convenience. Both the Cavalier and the Puritan elements in Whistler's character rejected any such ideal, so that he seemed to stand out from many of his English contemporaries by his ruthless egotism, and from many of his fellow artists in France because he had, after all, a code. There was something seventeenth-century in his nature which made him as much out of place in the England of Ruskin as in the France of Verlaine. The strains which made up Whistler's character may be observed plainly enough in the lives of some of his immediate forebears.

His grandfather, John Whistler, belonged to the Irish branch of the family, that is, the ultra-Protestant and Puritan branch. In his personal character he was a little wild. He ran away from home and enlisted in the army, a desperate step in the eighteenth century. He had, moreover, the bad taste to enlist in a regiment in which one of his kinsmen, Sir Kensington Whistler, already held a commission. Sir Kensington took immediate steps to have him removed to another regiment, and managed matters so well that his erring relative soon found himself on the way to the American colonies, under the command of General Burgoyne. He arrived in time to surrender at Saratoga.

It was, therefore, the purest chance that John Whistler ever went to America at all, but he seems to have liked what he saw there, for he was soon to settle there of his own free will. Returning to England with the remnants of Burgoyne's army, he became acquainted with the daughter of a certain Sir Edward Bishop, and fell in love with her. The family, not unnaturally, objected to a match between Anna Bishop and a penniless private soldier disbanded from a defeated army, and John Whistler persuaded the lady to elope with him. Finding England too unfriendly, the young couple sailed for America and settled at Hagerstown, in the State of Maryland.

John Whistler knew only one way of earning his living, and as he had once enlisted in the British Army, so he now enlisted in that of the United States. Promotion was easier than it would have been in England, and the young soldier rose in time to be brevet-major, and served in the War of 1812 against Great Britain. He retired from the army in 1815, and died two years later at Bellefontaine,

Missouri, leaving behind him fifteen children, of whom three were soldiers and three married to soldiers. The military tradition was very strong in the Whistler family.

One of the three soldier sons was born at Fort Wayne in 1800, and received the patriotic name of George Washington. He was educated first at a school in Kentucky, and later at West Point Military Academy, where he held some kind of official appointment.

His first wife was the daughter of an army surgeon, Dr. Foster Swift, and by her he had three children, of whom the daughter Deborah is the only one who need concern us here. When his first wife died, Major Whistler, as he had become by this time, married Anna Mathilda McNeill, a descendant of those McNeills of Skye who had emigrated to America as a clan, after the defeat of the Young Pretender.

The major, finding insufficient scope in the army for his talents as an engineer, resigned his commission in 1833 and set up in private practice. In the following year he was offered a post as engineer of locks and canals at Lowell, in Massachusetts, and it was here, shortly after his arrival, that the subject of the present study was born.

The boy was baptized at St. Anne's Church, Lowell, on November 9, 1834, with the names of James Abbott. The more romantic McNeill was not added, but this omission was remedied by Whistler later in life, just as he corrected the mistake of his birthplace. He was a Southerner

[ 19 ]

and a Celt, and he was determined that the world should know it.

It was natural enough that Lowell should hold small place in his affections, for when he was three years old the family removed to Stonington, in Connecticut, where Major Whistler was constructing new railroads. In spite of these activities, the atmosphere surrounding the family was one of eighteenth-century simplicity and quiet. The house on "Main Street" was of the old pattern, and the manners of its inhabitants cast in the ancient mold. In the frequent absence of her husband, Mrs. Whistler ruled the household with the strictness and impartiality of her austere creed. She was a rigid sabbatarian, and on Sundays all toys were put away, and all books but the Bible forbidden. The household was a nursery of the Old Testament virtues, strengthened, rather than impaired, by the family's strong military tradition.

A childhood passed in such surroundings is not always the harsh captivity that modern sentimentalists believe. The four boys were by no means unhappy, and if they subsequently fell away from their mother's teaching, they did so without recrimination, and with no hint in their attitude to her of anything but the utmost respect and affection. Whistler, indeed, like other intense individualists, developed in later life an almost idolatrous veneration for systems of discipline from which he had himself escaped.

The fourth son was not born until the family had removed once more, this time to Springfield, in Massachusetts. A yet longer journey was awaiting them, for in 1842 Major Whistler received an offer of twelve thousand dollars a year to build a railway between St. Petersburg and Moscow for the Emperor Nicholas I. He sailed for Europe the same year, and in 1843, finding himself established in Russia, sent for his family.

Such a journey by a woman with a young family would be no small undertaking even now; in the early forties of the last century it was an enterprise of magnitude. The voyage from Boston to Liverpool took seventeen days, but the travelers were able to rest for a fortnight with Mrs. Whistler's relations, who lived at Preston in Lancashire. Whistler was nine years old when he first set eyes on London, and his first view of Wapping and Gravesend must have been from the deck of the vessel which carried the family to Hamburg.

Here, modernity was left behind. No railway stretched toward the eastern frontier, and Mrs. Whistler and her party traveled to Lübeck and on to Travemünde by carriage and stagecoach, along roads little better than those which ran through Germany before the United States had come into existence. At Travemünde the party took ship once more and sailed for Kronstadt; but before the citadel could be reached, Whistler's baby brother died of seasickness, aggravated by the fatigue of the journey. As another

[ 21 ]

son had died in America before she left, Mrs. Whistler
had now only two sons, James and William, and her step-
daughter Deborah, who traveled with them.

In St. Petersburg a house was taken in the Galernaïa,
in the fashionable quarter near the Admiralty. The boys—
Jimmie was nearly ten—were delighted with the new
world opened to their view. They found themselves in
the very center of the most impressive part of the great
city. Almost opposite their front door was the principal
entrance to the military Académie Nicolas. A few steps
brought them to the Cathedral of St. Isaac, and a few more
to the Winter Palace, just rebuilt after its disastrous fire.
They walked with their governess in the wide "Perspec-
tives" radiating from the Admiralty, or in the cross-streets,
broad and somewhat empty, lined with monotonous but
brightly colored houses. It was more difficult to penetrate
to the poor quarters, where street vendors sold hot tea
and hydromel and every kind of salad, and where the
bright peasant costumes were still to be seen.

In the better streets, the carriages of the aristocracy
passed unceasingly, and occasionally those of the court
with grooms in scarlet livery. Almost everyone wore a
uniform of some kind, from generals to street sweepers,
from civil servants to schoolboys, and the military atmosphere of the place must have done something to reenforce
Whistler's inherited instincts. Indeed, St. Petersburg was
to have more effect upon his character, or rather upon the

[ 22 ]

formation of his mind, than is often realized. Much in Whistler's life and in his art becomes comprehensible if we remember that it was in a foreign capital that he (who was to spend the greater part of his life in foreign capitals) passed the most impressionable years of his childhood. The feeling of isolation, combined with a sense of belonging to a semi-military caste, one might almost say the sensation of being a distinguished foreigner,[1] was already present in his early days in St. Petersburg.

Even the visual aspect of the Russian capital had its effect upon his imagination. The blue mists which hang over a river with the lights of a great city glimmering through them, he had already learned to love on the banks of the Neva, when the Seine was still unknown to him, and the Thames no more than a passing glimpse in the middle of a long journey. His life-long ignorance of tree-form, his indifference to rural landscape as it is usually understood, may be traced back to his residence in St. Petersburg, as well as a certain austerity in his view of cities, his refusal of picturesque detail seen at close quarters. The former Russian capital is a city of straight lines and wide spaces, and its dignified urbanity did something to prepare him for the Georgian architecture of London, equally dignified in its more crowded fashion.

[1] W. Shaw Sparrow, in his reminiscences ("Memories of Life and Art"), makes the shrewd remark that it was often possible to get Whistler to do what you wanted if you took care to treat him as "a very sensitive foreign Power."

Whistler was a delicate little boy, and the first winter in Russia proved very trying. He suffered from severe rheumatic attacks which weakened his heart, and in the spring, when the thaw began, he was extremely liable to take cold. Mrs. Whistler, in her diary, contrasted his pale, sleeping face with the round cheeks of her other son, Willie, and feared that he might follow the child who had died on the journey. Even the summer in St. Petersburg was not very agreeable, for the nights were excessively short, and as the cafés remained open and the noise of vehicles in the fashionable quarters never ceased, it was difficult to get much sleep. The Whistlers therefore rented a country house on the Peterhof road in the spring of 1844, and there Jimmie picked up his strength.

The boys had a Swedish tutor as well as a governess, and made so much progress with foreign tongues that their mother made them read aloud to her from the Bible and from an English history book in order that they should not forget their own language.

In April, 1845, Jimmie was entered as a scholar of the Imperial Academy of Fine Arts in "the drawing class, heads from Nature." The academy was just on the opposite side of the Neva and could be seen from the upper bedroom windows of the Whistler house. Whistler had only to slip round the corner of the Galernaïa and cross the river by St. Isaac's bridge of boats, now swept away; but he was not long to enjoy his drawing lessons undisturbed, for, in the autumn of 1846, both he and his brother became boarders in the school of a certain M. Jourdan and were absent from home for a week at a time.

Mrs. Whistler had given birth to another son since her arrival in Russia, but he did not long survive. James, too, gave her renewed cause for anxiety. The close confinement of the boarding school did not suit him, and when he tried to get some healthy exercise by skating on the Neva, he was taken ill with another attack of rheumatism.

He was an invalid for six weeks in January and February, 1847, and his only comfort was a large volume of Hogarth's engravings, propped up before him on the bed.

The impressions of childhood (Whistler was now nearly thirteen) are extraordinarily difficult to efface. If there was one artist in the world for whom Whistler might be supposed in later life to have no sympathy, it was surely Hogarth; yet however far his own practice might stray, however much he might rail against "subject," however much he might insist on the purely decorative aspects of painting, he never wavered from his belief that Hogarth was the greatest English artist. Perhaps he was, but that Whistler thought so was an accident of his childhood rather than the considered judgment of his maturity.

In March, 1847, the emperor inspected the railway from Moscow to St. Petersburg, and hung round the neck of the successful engineer the Order of St. Anne. Major Whistler's work was not yet finished, but he had earned a holiday, and in the summer the whole family sailed for England and stayed with their friends at Preston. Here Deborah, now a grown woman, met a young surgeon named Francis Seymour Haden and married him. The family returned to St. Petersburg without her.

During the next winter, however, James was ill once more, this time with rheumatic fever, and he was scarcely better before cholera broke out in the Russian capital. Mrs. Whistler, terrified not at all for herself but only for her sons, brought them once more to England, where, at Shanklin in the Isle of Wight, James gradually recovered his strength. When he had done so Mrs. Whistler returned to Russia to be with her husband, leaving James with Seymour Haden and his wife, who had now moved to London and were living at 62 Sloane Street.

Whistler's previous glimpses of London had been tantalizingly short. Now, at the age of fourteen, he was to have almost a year in which to explore it. He took lessons with a clergyman and he went to children's parties, but he must often have wandered out alone, and it is not fantastic to suggest that he may even then have walked from Sloane Street into Chelsea and made his way to the river.

His father died of the effects of cholera in April, 1849. The emperor offered to have his sons educated in the school for court pages, but, her husband dead, there was nothing to keep Mrs. Whistler in Russia, and she decided to return to America with the remnants of her family. After a short stay in England they arrived back in New York in July, 1849, after an absence of six years.

The death of Major Whistler left his family comparatively poor; their income having shrunk from twenty thousand dollars a year to fifteen hundred dollars. But Mrs. Whistler, with the true Puritan spirit, determined that whatever economies were necessary the boys must complete their schooling. She settled at Pomfret, in Connecticut, in order to be near a good school, and Whistler resumed his interrupted studies. To these he was not very attentive, but what he lacked in industry he made up in charm. He was a tall, delicate youth, extremely handsome, with a thoughtful face and a mop of soft brown curls falling over his forehead. Yet his somewhat feminine appearance was belied by manly spirit. Whistler was always courageous, excessively so in later life, and never hesitated to plunge into conflict with boys or men twice his size. His was an extraordinarily well-balanced character without morbidity or introspection. The soul-searchings which distress and paralyze other adolescents passed him by. His will was as yet unformed, but it was never divided against itself, and this singleness was both his strength and his limitation.

His natural talent for drawing was already obvious, although such as have survived of the sketches and scribbles with which he covered his schoolbooks show no sign of any abnormal precocity. Of all his lessons he liked geography best, for then he could draw maps, and these maps were marvels of daintiness and delicacy. But at the beginning of the fifties, his school days proper were almost over.

With so strong a tradition in the family, it was natural that the young Whistler should regard a military career as the inevitable one. His father had been on the staff at West Point, and his friends had sufficient influence with the authorities to insure the young man's admittance to the famous military academy on July 1, 1851.

The great Confederate general, Robert E. Lee, then a colonel in the United States Army, became superintendent of the academy in the following year, and it was under him that the greater part of Whistler's three years at the academy was passed. The military atmosphere which had surrounded Whistler from his earliest days was here intensified, and in its intensified form he did not like it. It was one thing to admire the military bearing; quite another to submit to military discipline.

Among his companions he was popular, with the popularity of the amiable eccentric. His flowing locks earned him the nickname of "Curly," and his high-spirited courage made him respected. He had none of the other-worldliness which attracts persecution as the lamb attracts the wolf. The Shelleys of this life lie open to every wound; the Whistlers escape with a nickname, which they wear as a decoration.

It is odd how early in life a man's peculiarities appear.

[ 28 ]

At West Point, Whistler was already a dandy, a gourmet, and an amateur cook, and often risked serious punishment by his failure to dress like his comrades, and by his willingness to "break bounds" in order to go long distances for some especial delicacy such as buckwheat cakes, or oysters, or ice-cream. Such pranks only increased his popularity with his fellows, but the authorities of West Point looked upon his activities with a less friendly eye.

Destiny presides over the youth of famous men, inspiring them with a happy indifference toward all those studies which contribute nothing to their natural talent. Whistler's indifference to the curriculum at West Point was profound. He had sufficient quickness of wit to keep out of serious trouble, but his unpunctuality was, even then, habitual, and his individualism already pronounced. He was not born to be a soldier in a century when a commission was to be won only by the accumulation of masses of useless knowledge. "If silicon had been a gas, I should have been a major-general," he declared, when joking about his failure in chemistry; but we may well doubt whether even so great a derangement of the natural order would have made of Whistler a soldier. In the seventeenth century he might have been the leader of a squadron of cavalry (although his riding was terrible), or a captain of musketeers, have twirled ferocious mustachios with D'Artagnan, or bandied words, or blows, with Cyrano. But in a modern army he would have been ill at ease. Certainly every mess

[ 29 ]

in the United States should have offered up prayers of thankfulness that Whistler was not numbered among its junior officers. He would never have become a major-general, for he would have got himself cashiered as a lieutenant. He carried away from West Point little but that picturesque conception of honor which was to seem so singularly out of place in Victorian London.

Mrs. Whistler was naturally grieved at her son's failure to become an officer. However, Major Whistler had left the army to become a locomotive engineer; James could do the same. She immediately set about finding him a place in the locomotive works at Baltimore. Mr. Ross Winans, the owner of the works, was a friend, indeed a relation of the family, and the opening was a good one. But Whistler had no intention whatever of becoming an engineer. He walked through the office once or twice and made sketches on the other apprentices' drawing-boards. Baltimore pleased him sufficiently to be adopted as one of his birthplaces, but he had no liking for steam engines and no talent for engineering. He abandoned his second profession after less than six months' trial.

Instead of going home, he traveled to Washington, and with superb effrontery, called on Jefferson Davis, with the suggestion that the secretary of war, for such he was, should reinstate him at West Point or find him some other career suitable to his talents. Davis seems to have been impressed by the young man (Whistler was exactly twenty), and as it was impossible to readmit him to West Point, found him a post in the office of the Coastal Survey.

In any capital city Whistler expanded like a flower in the sun. Washington was then small enough, but a capital is all the better for being small. Its social life is more homogeneous, and to have penetrated one door is to have penetrated all. Some of the officials in Washington had known Whistler's father. The Russian attachés had known the family in St. Petersburg. Whistler's charm conquered the rest, and he soon had more invitations than he could accept. He dined with the British and Russian diplomats and even invited them back to his own small apartment, although he was at times so short of money that he had to pin back the tails of his frock coat to simulate the appearance of evening dress.

His salary was a dollar and a half a day, but he seldom arrived at the office in time for his attendance to count as a day's work. In January, 1855, the records credit him with six and one-half days, and in February with five and three-quarters. Even with a room at the modest sum of ten dollars a month he was sure to find himself in difficulties. His superiors showed him the utmost indulgence. Captain Benham, who was in charge of the Coastal Survey, and had known Whistler's father, asked one of the young man's fellow draftsmen to call for him in the morning, but the only result was that both arrived an hour and a half late. Even when he was in the office he did as little

[ 31 ]

as possible, spending his time sketching from the windows, or scribbling on the copperplates provided by the government.

Before the invention of photomechanical processes, charts and maps were reproduced by means of etching, the draftsman himself transferring the diagrams to the plate. This was the only part of his work which Whistler enjoyed. He learned the technique of etching very quickly. The delicacy required in the laying of the ground and the handling of the acid appealed to his fastidiousness, and the proficiency he acquired in the office of the Coastal Survey he never lost. From his third profession he carried away something which was to be useful to him all his life.

His dislike of any kind of study remained as strong as ever. He read but little, but somewhere or other he had picked up a copy of Henri Murger's "Scènes de la Vie de Bohême." It seemed to him the ideal life. To have an *appartement* in the Quartier Latin. to be impecunious but cheerful, to strike up friendships with eccentric characters, each a genius as yet unrecognized, to be intimate with models, to be familiar with the waiters at cafés, and, behind and beyond all this, to burn with an unquenchable devotion for art—such seemed to Whistler, as it has seemed to many young men, to be the only existence worthy of noble natures. Of his own talent he had no doubt; of his incapacity to follow any laborious routine even his friends were at last becoming convinced. He thought no more of

Washington; he had forgotten St. Petersburg. Paris became the only city of his dreams, the only place where he
knew he could be happy.

Even the festivities of Washington lost their savor, and
the Coastal Survey became an intolerable tyranny from
which his sole thought was to escape. His attendances became more and more irregular, until, as abruptly as he
had accepted the post, he offered his resignation in February, 1855. He journeyed back to Stonington to face the
disappointment of his mother at his third failure to make
a career.

The Whistlers held a family conference. His elder
brother George, who now took Major Whistler's place,
thought that James ought to go back to the locomotive
works at Baltimore and try to earn an honest living. This
the young man refused to do. He was of age and entitled
to choose for himself. He announced that he intended to
go to Paris to study art.

His family could, of course, have made things difficult,
as they had very little money, and Whistler himself was
penniless. But, very wisely, they decided to throw no
obstacles in his way. Instead, they bought him a ticket
to Europe and promised him three hundred and fifty dollars a year so long as he should need them. The Prodigal
Son pocketed the money and left the United States forever
in the summer of 1855.

He broke his journey in London and stayed once more

with the Hadens in Sloane Street. With his half-sister, Deborah, or Dasha, as she was called, he had always been a favorite, and he found her authoritative husband oddly sympathetic. Seymour Haden had himself a secret ambition to be an artist, although, with more determination or less vocation than Whistler, he had not allowed the desire to hinder his career. But he listened eagerly to his young relative's account of life in the Coastal Survey and was obviously interested in the technique of etching. He promised to call on him in Paris later in the year when he visited the Exhibition.

Whistler was full of high spirits. At last he was free, with money in his pocket and the world before him. He unpacked his best suit of white duck, probably the first the London streets had ever seen, got out his wide-brimmed straw hat with the floating ribbons, and with the arrogance of sudden wealth purchased a first-class ticket to Paris.

## CHAPTER II

### WHISTLER IN PARIS

IN the year 1855 the Second Empire was at its apogee.
All those French middle classes which had seen in
the troubles of 1848 the beginnings of another French
Revolution were united in their support of a government
that seemed to promise them prosperity and, if not peace,
at least profitable war. One of the first sights which greeted
a visitor to Paris would have been the immense queues of
people waiting outside the Ministry of Finance, eager to
subscribe to the new Government Loan.

Napoleon had scattered the streets of the city with
lights like a prodigal scattering jewels. There seemed to
be gas lamps everywhere, for Paris was earning its proud
title of *La Ville Lumière*. The time was the very center of
what has been called *Le siècle du Boulevard*. The new
avenues were full and animated; the frock coats and tall
hats of the men and their narrow trousers contrasted with
the billowy fulness of the women's skirts. On the fashionable promenades everyone knew everybody else; the
cafés were crowded and prosperity seemed universal.
There was hardly a murmur of that industrial discon-
tent which, suppressed in 1848, was to burst forth again

[ 35 ]

twenty years afterwards, and find its final tragedy in the Commune.

In 1855 all is tranquil. True, there is a war in Russia, but all is going well. The communiqués are every day more cheerful. Soon will come the glorious news of the capture of the Malakoff, and the fall of Sebastopol. The emperor is fulfilling his destiny by making France glorious abroad as well as at home. Absorbed as he is in foreign politics, he has not forgotten his duty to Culture. There is an international exhibition in Paris, intended to be even more epoch-making than the great exhibition in Hyde Park of four years before. Paris is crowded with royalties. The Imperial Guard with shining breastplates, nodding plumes, ferocious mustachios, ride up and down the new rue de Rivoli perpetually protecting the arrival or the departure of some foreign potentate—now Queen Victoria, now Victor Emmanuel of Sardinia.

When Whistler arrived at the Gare de Boulogne (now the Gare du Nord), he had very little knowledge of Paris, and did not know where to stay. But he had learned from "La Vie de Bohême" that art students could live only in the Quartier Latin, and he had a vague idea that in the very middle of this stood the Théâtre de l'Odéon. He called a fiacre and explained his wants to the driver: a lodging near the Odéon.

"*Je connais ça,*" said the man, and drove his cab in the direction of the left bank.

[ 36 ]

To the south bank of the river the activities of Baron Haussmann had not yet penetrated. The Latin Quarter was almost as it had been in Murger's youth. It was the unspoiled playground still of Schaunard and Marcel. There were tumbledown houses with neglected gardens between the Sorbonne and the Luxembourg; there was no Boulevard St. Germain, no Boule' Miche'. Semirural streets radiated from the Place St. Sulpice, and in the square itself stood a strange erection, half cage, half sty, in which a real wild boar was kept.

In the middle of this untouched region stood an immense old-fashioned house with nearly a hundred rooms. A porte-cochère, on each side of which was a *café-billard,* led into a neglected courtyard, and at the far end of this was a large dining-room or restaurant, where the inhabitants of the house took their meals in common. The whole place was dilapidated and dirty, but Whistler did not mind. The porte-cochère of the Hôtel Corneille was the gateway of a new life.

He was not long in making friends. The hotel was occupied by an ever-shifting population of medical students and art students, and among the latter in 1855 was Lamont, the Laird in "Trilby," and the future author of "Trilby" himself. Du Maurier, then a tall, attractive youth with a slim figure, square shoulders, and the first hint of a mustache, had an eye for the picturesque, and Whistler's hat and long curls could not pass unnoticed. Lamont was

[ 37 ]

friendly too, and shared rooms with Whistler for a time, and the group of three was soon swelled by the arrival of Poynter [1] and, a little later, of Armstrong.[2]

All these friends had come to Paris to become painters, and the first question for them to decide was the choice of a master. Du Maurier, Poynter, and Whistler chose to work under Gleyre, who, in a studio which he had inherited from Delaroche and was afterwards to hand over to Gérôme, taught a large number of French and foreign students all that was unimportant in the method of Ingres. He told his pupils that black was the basis of tone, and this Whistler never forgot. But he seems to have learned little else in Gleyre's studio, for he hardly ever went there.

*La vie de bohême* enthralled him, and he even took pains to make his life more bohemian than he need have done. Haden kept his promise and came over to Paris for the Exhibition. His friends, the Thackerays, who were also over, invited Whistler to dinner, and as the latter had pawned his dress-suit, he borrowed one for the occasion from Lamont. Fortunately, for the sake of the story, the Laird's shoes would not fit, and Whistler was compelled to search the corridors of the Hôtel Corneille until he found a suitable pair, complaining bitterly the while of their inelegant shape. New gloves he procured by making love to the salesgirl in the glove shop.

[1] Later Sir Edward Poynter, President of the Royal Academy.
[2] Thomas Armstrong, afterwards C.B. and Director of the South Kensington Museum, now the Victoria and Albert.

He still had all his old fondness for social life, and there was an added pleasure in it against the bohemian background. The officials of the American Embassy used to invite him out, and, as an American citizen, he even procured invitations to the balls at the Tuileries, to the envious amazement of the Englishmen who would never have dreamed of using Lord Cowley as Whistler used Judge Mason, the American minister. Whistler delighted in these social functions. It was delicious to move, the disguised bohemian, among creatures of another world, and even more delicious to return to the Latin Quarter. It made him feel like a prince traveling incognito.

His intimacy with the English students, however, did not slacken, and he shared rooms with Poynter for a time. When the Hôtel Corneille was closed owing to the bankruptcy of its proprietor, Poynter took a studio in the rue Jacob, and Whistler set up house with a French bank clerk named Aubert. Perhaps he was already finding the stolidity of the English too much for him.

When Armstrong, Du Maurier, Lamont, and Poynter shared a studio at 53 rue Notre Dame des Champs, then a street of little two-storied houses amid gardens and trees, Whistler did not join them. He had no taste for their strenuous amusements, shared none of their enthusiasm for gymnastic exercises. The kind of life they led has been described for all time in the pages of "Trilby":

"A trapeze, a knotted rope and two parallel cords, supporting each ring, depended from a huge beam in the ceiling, and on the walls the plaster casts of arms and legs, Dante's face and Michelangelo's Leda were interspersed with foils, fencing masks, and boxing gloves." The occupants of the studios divided their time between painting and swinging Indian clubs, boxing with one another or indulging in strenuous horse-play. In fact, the afternoon was healthily spent in athletic and gymnastic exercises, till dinner-time, just as if the young men had been safely at Oxford or Cambridge instead of in the Quartier Latin.

"And you hobnobbed with models, male and female, students of law and medicine, painters and sculptors, workmen and blanchisseuses and grisettes, and found them very good company, and most improving to your French. . . . And the evening was innocently wound up with billiards, cards or dominoes, at the Café du Luxembourg opposite; or at the Théâtre du Luxembourg, in the Rue de Madame, to see funny farces with screamingly droll Englishmen in them; or, still better, at the Jardin Bullier (la Closerie des Lilas), to see the students dance the cancan . . . or, best of all, at the Théâtre de l'Odéon, to see Fechter and Madame Doche in the 'Dame aux Camélias.' "

"Trilby" first appeared as a serial in Harper's Monthly Magazine for January, 1894, nearly forty years after the events it sets out to describe. Whistler was at first included among the characters, under the name of Joe Sibley, but not appreciating the rôle allotted to him, he protested to

WHISTLER AND DU MAURIER IN
1860: *By George Du Maurier. Punch,*
XXXIX, *p. 140.*

THE IDLE AND THE INDUSTRI-
OUS APPRENTICE *(Whistler and
Poynter): By George Du Maurier.
Harper's Magazine,* LXXXVIII, *p.* 579.

the publishers so energetically that he disappeared altogether from the story in book form. It is of some interest
to disinter the offending passage now only to be found
in the pages of the bound volumes of Harper's, for if there
is a certain asperity in it, there is also considerable penetration, the penetration given to those who have been
friends and are so no longer:

Then there was Joe Sibley, the idle apprentice,
the King of Bohemia, *le roi des truands,* to whom
everything was forgiven, as to François Villon, "à
cause de ses gentillesses."

Always in debt, like Svengali; like Svengali, vain,
witty, and a most exquisite and original artist; and
also eccentric in his attire (though clean), so that
people would stare at him as he walked along—which
he adored! But, unlike Svengali, he was genial,
caressing, sympathetic, charming; the most irresistible
friend in the world as long as his friendship lasted—
but that was not forever.

The moment his friendship left off, his enmity
began at once. Sometimes this enmity would take the
simple and straightforward form of trying to punch
his ex-friend's head; and when the ex-friend was too
big, he would get some new friend to help him. And
much bad blood would be caused in this way—though
very little was spilt. And all this bad blood was not
made better by the funny things he went on saying
through life about the unlucky one who had managed
to offend him—things that stuck forever. . . .

He is now perched on such a topping pinnacle (of fame and notoriety combined) that people can stare at him from two hemispheres at once; and so famous as a wit that when he jokes (and he is always joking) people laugh first, then ask what it was he was joking about.

Obviously, the portrait is not without malice. Du Maurier had suffered at Whistler's hands like all his friends, and the very form of the passage quoted shows that he was thinking of the maturer Whistler rather than of the mere boy he had known in Paris.

Yet Whistler was much more intimate with the Englishmen than he was afterwards willing to admit. He was a fairly constant visitor to the studio and as welcome as any, except, perhaps, Aleco Ionides. Ionides was not an artist and did little but sit in an armchair "coloring" his pipe; but he was to prove a useful friend in London a few years later. Whistler seemed to be doing almost as little. In the drawing made by Du Maurier of "Ye Societie of Our Ladye in the Fieldes" (*i.e.* Notre Dame des Champs), Whistler is represented with his feet on the mantelpiece, his long ringlets falling over his eyes.[3]

He made no progress as a painter, but his interest in etching was as great as ever. He tried to arouse the enthusiasm of his friends and even proposed a kind of etching club to be called "Plawd," an anagram on the initial letters

[3] Reproduced in "Thomas Armstrong, A Memoir" (1912), p. 136.

of the names of Poynter, Lamont, Armstrong, himself and Du Maurier. The scheme proposed by Whistler was that each member of the club should etch a plate, choosing his own subject, and that the five etchings produced should be sent to a "literary bloke" in England in order that he might weave a story round them and make a book out of it. Whistler's notion of the functions of literary men was not very exalted even then.

Although the project came to nothing, it is a proof, if proof were needed, of a considerable degree of intimacy, and in the feasts and impromptu concerts at the studio he joined readily enough. Du Maurier had a passion and a genuine talent for music. He had an excellent voice also, and sang the airs from "Trovatore," then the rage in Paris, as well as a number of songs which he had picked up in the *cafés chantants* of the Quarter. Whistler had no voice, or very little, but he sometimes chanted some of the Negro melodies which he had heard in America.

Of the other amusements of his English friends, he was frankly contemptuous. He thought a gentleman should not descend to fisticuffs,[4] and dumb-bells seemed just waste of energy. We may be sure, too—if his subsequent opinions on English food prove anything—that he did not very often accompany Armstrong and the rest to the little English tavern in the rue Royale where they went every Saturday night to eat chops and drink beer.

[4] He was to change this opinion later, and even to take lessons from a professional pugilist who lived behind the Regent Quadrant.

[ 43 ]

To Poynter and his friends, he seemed to be merely wasting his time, and when the day came for Poynter as president of the Royal Academy to pronounce an oration on the death of Whistler, a whole lifetime of achievement on the part of the latter had not effaced from the president's mind his early impression of "The Idle Apprentice."

But Whistler had not come to Paris to work all the morning in a studio like a schoolboy, take exercise like a schoolboy every afternoon, and pass his evenings in Anglo-Saxon company. He seems to have been much more mature than his friends and to have plunged into the life of the Quarter with greater zest. How different the same district, at the same period, may appear to different eyes! To Poynter it was as harmless as Poynter's paintings, to Zola it was like life in Zola's novels, and to Whistler it was something between the two. He did not shut his eyes to its squalor, but he plunged gaily into the exhilarating current of a life freed from the petty restrictions of West Point and Washington, free also from the dread of absolute penury.

The Quartier Latin in the middle fifties was gayer and more corrupt than it had been in Murger's youth, but it was not yet overrun with sightseers and sensation-hunters. Murger and others had made it self-conscious, so that its life could be enjoyed with an added zest, but it was not yet the shoddy fake which artistic quarters become so very rapidly in the modern world.

[ 44 ]

There was plenty of amusement. The students' balls were crowded and were visited not only by students but by ladies of both the beau- and the demi-monde from the right bank. Whistler was there almost every night, and as a natural consequence, did not rise till eleven o'clock in the morning, when the session at Gleyre's was almost over. The rest of the day he sat in cafés, sketching. Unknown to himself, he was already imbued with the doctrine of the realists.

Women played an important part in the life of the Latin Quarter, and the vast majority of them were of the kind immortalized in the literature of romanticism under the name of "grisettes." The *grande cocotte* is the typical heroine of the Second Empire, but if she visited the students' balls, she did so because of a whim, or to escape the boredom of living with a diplomat or a minister. On the left bank of the river the ideals of the thirties still held good, and the grisette ruled supreme. All the week she sewed lingerie, or sold tobacco, or worked as a modiste. On Sunday she was free to accompany her student-lover in the horse-omnibus to Ranelagh or to Belleville, a quarter of Paris which still had some pretensions to its name. If it rained she devoured oranges in the gallery of a cheap theater, and wept copiously at the melodrama enacted upon the stage. She shared a momentary prosperity with gaiety and abandonment, and supported a too frequent poverty with good humor and fortitude. Like Murger's Mimi, she

[ 45 ]

was sometimes consumptive; like Musset's Mimi, she had only one dress. Like both, she had a heart of gold. Best of all, although she went to church quite often, she hardly expected to be led to the altar.

For most young men *la vie de bohême* is at some period of their existence the only paradise in which they still believe, a paradise inhabited by a fluttering cloud of grisettes, each transfigured by the light of imagination into something part houri and part guardian angel, part playmate and part odalisk.

Whistler was essentially the romantic, the submerged romantic who has grown impatient with "the far country" and the "once upon a time." The first romantics were historians and orientalists. The second brought romanticism nearer home, and Murger in particular made a nineteenth-century metropolis its fairy palace and its closed garden. Whistler had not come to Paris to be an English schoolboy, and the impersonal *bonhomie* of his fellow students was beyond his comprehension. The very femininity of his own nature desired a more intimate friendship, a warmer response, a relationship in which the small change of the intellect played no part at all. Besides, he was a man of the world, a cosmopolitan already, and it was inevitable that he should seek a mistress, and equally inevitable that he should find her among the grisettes.

The grisette of the fifties was more sophisticated than her sister of twenty years before. She was not only the subject of romanticism; she was herself its victim. She not only appeared in the works of Alfred de Musset; she read them. One little modiste was indeed famous in the Quarter for her devotion to the poet. She carried a volume of his verses about with her always and declaimed them to her acquaintance whenever opportunity offered.

> Poet, take your lute; the wine of youth
> Bubbles this night within the godhead's veins . . .

She sang, too, as all good grisettes should, and one of her songs has been recorded by Armstrong, who knew her well.

> Voulez vous savoir, savoir,
> Comment les artistes aiment?
> Ils aiment si artistement,
> Ils sont de si artistes gens.

> *Spoken:*
> Qu'ils s'en vont tout en disant:
> "Voulez vous venir chez moi, Mademoiselle?
> Et je ferai votre portrait."

> *Refrain:*
> Ramenez vos moutons, bergères,

> *Sung:*
> Ramenez vos moutons des champs.[5]

[5] Thomas Armstrong, C.B., "A Memoir" (1912), p. 192. The following is a free translation:

> Would you know, yes, know
> How artists love? They invoke

Whistler at least "made her portrait." He etched the girl with extraordinary delicacy and insight. The sad little face, with its mixture of charm and earnestness, the prim dress, the untidy hair, all combine to produce a character study already masterly in its penetration.

He lived with her for two years in the rue St. Sulpice. Her name was Eloïse, but he called her Fumette, and she was known in the Quarter as *la Tigresse* on account of her violent temper. Once, when he arrived at their lodgings, he found that she had torn up all his drawings in a fit of rage or jealousy. Whistler broke down and cried. Then, when he had recovered a little, he went out to the café, met two of his friends, and, like many another man in despair over a woman, made himself quite drunk. With the drowning of his sorrows, his gaiety returned, and he persuaded his companions to watch the night out in one of the little restaurants near the Halles. Unfortunately, none of the three had any money, so Whistler knocked up an American acquaintance named Lucas, and demanded a

Love with such utter artistry,
They are such artistic folk.

*Spoken:*
That they go off saying:
"Won't you come to my place, Mademoiselle?
I'll do your portrait."

*Refrain:*
Bring back your sheep, shepherdesses,

*Sung:*
Bring back your sheep from the fields.

loan. Lucas, seeing the borrower's condition, would give him nothing; but the adventurers supped none the less, while Whistler spoke of challenging Lucas to a duel. The two friends fell asleep in the restaurant, like true bohemians putting off the inevitable reckoning till the morrow, and when they awoke, a miracle had happened. Whistler had other American friends besides Lucas, and from one of them he had extracted several hundred francs. The bill was paid, and the three started joyfully homeward, and, as they passed one of their familiar cafés, who should be seated there, eating his breakfast, but the careful Lucas! But with the morning sanity had returned, and Whistler had forgotten the duel. He had realized, too, that his ménage with Fumette could not last. He had heard all her songs and all her recitations, and was tired of her uncertain temper. She drifted off to live with a musician and, later, took the road to Buenos Ayres and died there. A pure romantic, such as no longer exists.

He etched the portrait, also, of another woman with whom he was on terms more or less intimate, a cocotte named Finette who danced the cancan at the Bal Bullier. She must indeed have been more dancer than cocotte, for she danced the cancan well enough to be offered an engagement in London. Théodore Duret, Whistler's first biographer, calls her "a creole of easy virtue." Her elegance and sophistication are in striking contrast to the somewhat pathetic soulfulness of the little modiste.

[ 49 ]

It was not only with women that Whistler's knowledge of the language and his charming manners were of advantage. He got to know a great many of the native male students with whom his eccentricity passed unnoticed, and who saw nothing astonishing in the fact that a man who had some money to spend should spend it instead of settling down to work. On the rare occasions when he attended at Gleyre's he fell in with an Alsatian named Dabo, and in one of the cafés of the Quarter, he struck up a friendship with the little known painter Ernest Delannoy, which lasted for some years.

The only way by which the art student could make any money was by copying pictures. If he was fortunate, he might get a commission to copy a picture in the Louvre; but if not, he had to fall back on the "Stations of the Cross." There was a fairly constant demand for these necessary pieces of church furnishing and, in the days before cheap color reproductions, the curé of a poor church was willing to buy hand-painted copies of the scenes of the Passion if only they were cheap enough. There were shops (relates Armstrong) in the rue Bonaparte and the rue des Saints Pères where canvases could be obtained with the outlines of the required compositions already printed on them. These canvases were given out to young artists who returned them as finished pictures, receiving seven francs for each. As some of the canvases were nearly six feet long, the money was not easily earned.

Whistler was more fortunate. Not only had he an allowance from home, but friends from Washington or Stonington were continually searching him out. From the latter place came Captain Williams, or Stonington Bill, who got Whistler to paint his portrait, and was so pleased with it that he commissioned him to copy as many pictures as he liked for twenty-five dollars each. "I copied," said Whistler in later life, "a picture, I cannot remember whom it was by, of a snow scene, with a horse and a soldier standing by it and another in the snow at his feet; a second of St. Luke, with his halo and draperies, a third of a woman holding up a child toward a barred window and a man seen looking through the bars; and a fourth of an inundation. I have no doubt I made something very interesting out of them." Interesting or not, the pictures he copied serve to show that his talent was as yet totally undirected. In any case, he seems to have been paid for at least two of them, for it is recorded that the sudden wealth of two hundred and fifty francs made him think of taking a holiday, one of those sketching tours which the wealthier students were always taking. Why should he not accept Dabo's invitation to visit him in Alsace? He asked Ernest to go with him, and the bohemian accepted. The two set out with a minimum of luggage, Whistler in the thin pumps which he wore all his life, even for country walking, his wide-brimmed straw hat, and a knapsack of copperplates. Gleyre had not taught him how to paint, but he

[ 51 ]

had not forgotten the technique of etching he had learned at Washington.

The two travelers made their way, probably by train, to Nancy, and thence to Lunéville and Saverne, or Zabern, where Dabo lived. Saverne is a dull little town at the foot of a spur of the Vosges, and it is unlikely that Whistler found much to interest him in what antiquities it possesses. But in the streets one evening he was struck by the deserted aspect of the place, and, drawing a piece of grounded copper from his packet, scratched the lines of one of the most masterly of his early plates. It is a view of a street, with threatening, sinister houses leading on into an ominous patch of darkness, a high street-lamp illuminating the row of blind façades. The plate was not bitten at once, but carefully wrapped up and placed in the knapsack when the travelers continued their journey.

It is probable that they went to Strassburg and descended the Rhine by boat, for a tourist service was already being organized, but the journey was still a complicated one, for the unification of Germany was yet in the future and it was necessary to have a whole string of visas on one's passport and to understand the value of Prussian thalers and imperial florins. This constant changing of money, in addition to the ordinary expenses of traveling, devoured Whistler's small capital sooner than he had expected, and at Cologne he found himself without a penny.

[ 52 ]

There was no one in the town to whom he could apply. The nearest American consul was at Aachen. Whistler wrote frantic letters to Seymour Haden and to his friends in Paris, but a fortnight passed and no answer came. The two young artists were on good terms with the landlord of their inn, and Whistler had made an etching of his daughter, Gretchen. But as the etching was as yet unproved, Herr Schmitz could hardly be expected to appreciate it, and when Whistler proposed that he should accept all the copperplates in pledge for a fortnight's lodging he was extremely dubious. However, he was persuaded at last; the precious etchings were left behind, and Whistler and Ernest set out to walk back to Paris. Their sole wealth was one silver groschen (about one and sixpence) which the maid at the inn slipped into Whistler's hand when he said good-by.

To pay for food and lodging they were compelled to draw portraits in the villages they passed through, and Whistler has left a very vivid etching of himself at work surrounded by a group of German-looking youths gazing at him in wonder. To add to their troubles, the weather was abominable, but they tramped on steadily toward the Belgian frontier.

Whistler's later accounts of this adventure were perhaps a little highly colored, and we may probably discount the story that the two artists joined a troop of traveling musicians and played the big drum for them at country fairs. At Aachen, Whistler got an advance of fifty francs from the American consul; but the distance of Aachen from Cologne is fifty miles at most, and the two young men should have been able to walk as much in three or four days. From Whistler's story, as reported by Pennell, the reader would gather that they were on the road for months.

Fifty francs was almost enough to take them both to Paris and at Liège Ernest managed to get twenty more from the French consul. They arrived back in Paris tramp-like enough to satisfy the most romantic, and Whistler immediately sent off money to Cologne and retrieved his precious coppers.

He had now etched sufficient plates to be able to think of publication; but first it was necessary for the etchings to be printed. Whistler was fortunate, for Paris was, in the late fifties, the only place in the world where etchings could be printed satisfactorily, and the only man, even in Paris, who could give a bitten plate all its value was Auguste Delâtre.

This interesting man had been born in Paris in 1822, and at the age of twelve had entered his father's workshop to learn the business of printing copperplates. Not only was his work extremely skilful, but it came at exactly the right moment, for what is known as the Etching Revival was just beginning.

Delacroix had been an innovator in etching as in painting, and although his plates are somewhat slight and hasty, perhaps for that very reason they were the more useful in freeing etching from its subservience to line engraving. Daubigny's portfolios had appeared at the beginning of the fifties; Corot and Millet both etched, but their etching is comparatively unimportant. Bracquemond [6] and Charles Jacque were to have more influence, especially on Whistler.

Jacque, who was born in 1813, had been a soldier until about 1835. In 1848 he was with Millet and Théodore Rousseau at Barbizon, but he had already developed his own manner. He etched farmyard and other rural scenes and had so great a fondness for drawing pigs that the Goncourts called him *le maître au cochon.*

Delâtre had worked for him as a printer since the early forties, and it may have been in Delâtre's workshop in the rue St. Jacques that Whistler saw Charles Jacque's work, for see it he undoubtedly did. The close similarity between Jacque's "Récureuse" and Whistler's "La Marchande de Moutarde" (finer as Whistler's work is) can hardly be denied; and there is a close parallel between the treatment of the figure in Jacque's "Ma Petite Fille" and Whistler's "Annie, Seated." [7]

Delâtre's shop was a recognized meeting-place for

[6] Bracquemond had little, if any, influence on Whistler's etching; but it was he who introduced the American to Japanese art. See p. 112.

[7] Mr. Martin Hardie, of the Victoria and Albert Museum, was the first to point this out. See "The Art of Etching," by E. S. Lumsden (London, 1925), p. 295.

etchers, and it is extremely likely that he not only saw Jacque's work there but met the artist himself. He also met Alphonse Legros, who had begun to etch in the year Whistler came to Paris; but it is very doubtful if he ever knew one of the most interesting etchers the world has ever produced, for between 1856 and 1859 Charles Meryon was away from Paris and for part of the time was shut up in an asylum.

Whistler always professed the greatest contempt for Meryon's etchings, yet in one respect at least he was indebted to him, for Meryon taught Delâtre to print for him with an ink made of very thin (perhaps unburnt) oil. The method was imparted by Delâtre to Whistler, and the delicacy of the latter's printing is at least partly due to it.[8] Whistler's work was issued as "Twelve Etchings from Nature," with the address of Haden's house in London and of Delâtre's workshop in Paris.

The expenses of redeeming the plates and of having them printed had left him poorer than ever, and he returned to copying pictures in the Louvre. He copied the nude figure of Angelica chained to the rock in Ingres's picture, and a group in Couture's "Romains de la Décadence." "The painting of the former," relates Armstrong,

[8] "The Art of Etching," by E. S. Lumsden (London, 1925), p. 281. For those who care for etching it is interesting to follow the tradition of fine printing as it passes from Delâtre to Whistler, from Whistler to Frederick Goulding, from Goulding to Sir Frank Short, and so to all the etchers trained under him.

WHISTLER IN 1859: *From an im=
pression in the Victoria and Albert
Museum.*

FUMETTE: *From an impression in the*
*Victoria and Albert Museum.*

"was not a bit like that of Ingres, for it was done in a thin, transparent manner, with no impasto and hardly enough paint to cover the canvas. . . . When we reproached Jimmie with not putting more paint on, he replied that the price he was to be paid would not run to much more than good linseed oil, for he was to have only one hundred francs apiece for the copies."

Whistler knew from his own attempts how difficult it is to make a good copy, so difficult that good copyists are even rarer than good artists, and it was his fortune to stumble on one of the best copyists that have ever lived. He was walking in the Louvre shortly after his return from Germany, when he saw a young man at work before "The Marriage Feast at Cana." Whistler stopped and, with charming spontaneity, began to praise the copy. The shy young artist was pleased and asked Whistler's name. Whistler told him.

"My name," said the other man, "is Fantin-Latour."

Among young men at least, friendship at first sight is no impossibility, and Fantin and Whistler seemed to become intimate at once. Whistler was charming, with that almost feminine fascination which he could exert on people when he chose. "After all, he is captivating," said Fantin many years later, just as one might talk of a difficult mistress. Fantin suggested, somewhat timidly, that they should dine together, and, shutting up his paint-box, led the way to the left bank.

[ 57 ]

The place to which he conducted Whistler was in all probability the Café Guerbois, where Fantin and his friends already formed a recognized group. Here the talk was all of one man, Courbet, whom every young revolutionary in Paris regarded as his master.

"Where are you studying?"

"Under Gleyre."

"You are wasting your time. Gleyre thinks he is carrying on the tradition of Ingres because he paints the nude. So does Couture with his vast paraphernalia like 'Les Romains de la Décadence.' It is not the decadence of the Romans, it is the decadence of Art."

"You are wasting your time under Gleyre." Whistler reflected with satisfaction that at least he had wasted very little. But who was Courbet, the apostle to all these young men of a new revelation?

Gustave Courbet was born in 1819 at Ornans in the department of Doubs, of a family not of peasants but of fairly prosperous rural proprietors in whom a revolutionary attitude was traditional. He came to Paris in 1839 and soon tired of his academic masters and carved out a new road for himself in "L'Homme à la Pipe," which was shown in the Salon of 1844. His uncompromising attitude made him many enemies, and his work was for several years excluded from the annual exhibitions. These rebuffs, however, served only to increase his influence, and by 1853 he had become a center of revolutionary movements both in art and in politics. His political activities, his friendship with Proudhon, and his part in the Commune of 1871 do not concern us here. In art he was in revolt both against the degenerate followers of Ingres and against the uninspired disciples of Delacroix. The classical ideal of the one had become a mere excuse for the academic nude, and the romantic subject matter of the other, while it had inspired a whole school of excellent illustrators, in easel-painting had lapsed into anecdote. The kind of art which found favor with the public of the Second Empire was pseudo-oriental, pseudo-classical, or pseudo-eighteenth-century.

Art, like Antæus, can renew its strength only by fresh contact with the earth, by drawing new inspiration from life as it is. This contact, this inspiration, Courbet was able to supply. By birth and temperament he was devoid of all the fatal superficial refinement which is art's perpetual danger. He had the healthy sensuality of the man of the soil rather than the seductive elegance which the town-bred artist often finds so easy.

He proclaimed the doctrine of "realism," as almost all reformers have done before or since, but, fortunately, his realism was of the healthy kind, neither photographic nor niggling, and, while it saved him from the danger which threatened his contemporaries, did not lead him into any new excesses.

The cry of realism has been raised so often in painting that it is worth pausing a moment to try to understand what is meant by so curious a term. It was in the name of realism that Ruskin praised Turner, and that the Pre-Raphaelites sought to paint every leaf in the foreground of their pictures. It was in the name of realism that they struggled with a pedantic interpretation of local color, to the sacrifice of any reality of general effect. It was in the name of realism that Zola was to defend the early canvases of Manet.

Realism, it need hardly be said, is a delusion, a will-o'-the-wisp. Conventions are essential to any art, not least to painting, which relies on a whole system of general agreements in order to represent a world of three dimensions on a canvas that has but two. Truth of local color means the sacrifice of relation in space; deliberately pedantic modeling means the loss of all truth of atmosphere. The artist must select in order to give even the illusion of reality, and when he has done that he has scarcely begun to be a painter. Courbet's "realism" never interfered with his overmastering sense of design. The "Burial at Ornans" is a most skilful piece of arbitrary construction, although the rhythm was both too simple and too subtle to be visible to many of his contemporaries. What Courbet's doctrine stood for was an acceptance of life as it is, of men in long trousers and tall hats. It was a proclamation of the dignity of life (even of modern life) and the denial of that easy escape to an earlier or an imagined world which ends, sooner or later, in a shriveling of the imagination, and the mere accumulation of bric-à-brac.

[ 60 ]

The studio of Courbet was already a legend. He had taken a vast room in the rue Hautefeuille, an old chapel of a Premonstratensian monastery, with an authentic Louis XIII staircase, and here he lived and worked in a romantic disorder, half squalid and half luxurious. Here came Bonvin, the genre painter, his earliest friend in Paris, Corot and Daumier, Duranty, the critic, Barye, the sculptor, Champfleury and Théodore de Banville. Here Baudelaire lived in the days of his extremest poverty, and here came Schanne, the familiar of Courbet, but better known to the world as Schaunard, for it is under that name that he figures in "La Vie de Bohême." Here, too, came Murger himself.

Whistler must have realized that he had reached the fringe of the Paris he had dreamed of, yet in his wildest dreams he had never imagined that Schaunard was a real person, as real as his creator Murger and not much more fantastic.

Was it possible to meet Courbet? Fantin assured him that nothing was easier, whenever Courbet was in Paris. Whistler would probably have met him sooner had he not been out of the capital for so long in recent years. Courbet, regarded as a dangerous man by his contemporaries, was flattered by the attentions he received from younger artists and inclined to be friendly toward them. Whistler went to see him and returned, saying: "He's a great man! He's a great man!"

The link between the master and Fantin's group was

Bonvin. Bonvin was a not very successful painter in the style of the minor Dutch masters. All his life he was unfortunate, and he died blind and a pauper. But he was a man of kindly and winning disposition, with a real appreciation of the work of other artists, even though they were much younger than he and as yet unrecognized. He allowed his young friends to draw and paint from the model in his studio, and Whistler joined the group, eager to make up for the time he had lost under Gleyre. Courbet acted as a kind of unofficial instructor, coming to the studio whenever he could and criticizing the young men's work. It was here Whistler had the only systematic training he ever received. He regretted in after life that it had not been longer, for he never learned to draw hands and feet with any certainty, and his imperfect knowledge of the human figure caused him a thousand difficulties. In a moment of discouragement, he even lamented to Fantin that he had not studied under Ingres.

Whistler realized that at last he had found what he had been looking for so long—a group of artists with whom he could work in sympathy and from whom he could learn something about painting. He had, indeed almost unwittingly, stumbled upon a group which we can now recognize to have been in the great central tradition of French painting, the group which was to act as a forcing-house for impressionism and which was, therefore, one of the main sources of modern art.

[ 62 ]

In obedience to the new doctrine, and also to the natural preference he had already shown in his etchings, the subject matter of his first original paintings was drawn from the life around him, from the cafés, and from the Bal Bullier. At the door of the latter, in the late fifties, stood the familiar figure of an old woman selling flowers. She was well educated, with some literary gift, but a series of misfortunes of one kind and another had reduced her from comfortable circumstances to all the miseries of street-hawking. The students called her la Mère Gérard. Emerging from the *bal* on one occasion, Whistler was struck by her picturesque appearance and asked her to sit for him. She consented, and the ill-assorted pair became, if not close friends, at least constant companions. He provided for her modest wants as well as he could, and even took her into the country on picnics and excursions. She had a shrewd sarcastic philosophy, and Whistler no doubt enjoyed the sharpness of her tongue. He even appreciated the caustic, "One more rascal the less," with which she greeted the quite erroneous news of his own untimely death.

The full-length etched portrait of the old woman is one of the best of his early plates, and his first original painting shows the same weather-beaten, somewhat bitter face. It was a heavily impasted canvas, owing much to Courbet, and the master praised it warmly when he saw it in Bonvin's studio. Whistler found another down-at-heel model in the person of an old vendor of chamber-pots. He painted him as "L'Homme à la Pipe," and the whole arrangement of the picture is strongly reminiscent of Courbet's portrait of himself with a pipe in his mouth.

Somewhere about 1859 Whistler began to consider that his student days had lasted long enough. He wanted to begin his professional career as a painter and he realized, only too clearly, how difficult it would be to dispose of his work in France. Perhaps England offered a better market.

The Haden establishment in Sloane Street was always open to him whenever he cared to stay there. His visits became more frequent, and sometimes he brought his young friends with him. Fantin and Legros were almost as welcome as himself, but "Ernest" was a complete savage with a total ignorance of table manners. Whistler, who had now outgrown the squalid stage of his bohemianism, felt his friendship toward Delannoy beginning to cool. He sympathized with his brother-in-law's horror, for he had once left his lodgings in Paris in charge of the bohemians, and on his return had found a state of dirt and disorder difficult to describe, and even more difficult to remedy. His natural fastidiousness was reasserting itself after a long eclipse.

By the public, Fantin, Legros, and Whistler himself were regarded as realists, but if the term means little when applied to Courbet it means less when applied to them. So far from working with their eyes on the object, as they were popularly supposed to do, two at least of them, Fantin and Legros, had absorbed the doctrine of the famous drawing master, Lecoq de Boisbaudran, whose system consisted essentially in the cultivation of the memory and, therefore, in the elimination of unnecessary detail. This system, Whistler, although he had not learned the method at first hand, was afterward to bring to a high pitch of perfection.

In the early part of the careers of young artists, these fine distinctions are scarcely visible to themselves, still less to the general public; and Whistler and the rest were very well content, in the late fifties, to be considered as the disciples of Courbet.

Courbet, however, was not the only source of inspiration. Young artists in Paris in the late fifties were conscious of another influence also: that of Spain. Goya had had little effect upon the French painters after his own generation, but to the men of the mid-nineteenth century it came as a shock of discovery to find the Spanish master as modern as themselves. And behind Goya stood the somber and impressive figure of Velasquez.

It became the dream of both Fantin and Whistler to go to Spain, and Legros shared their enthusiasm. None of them at the moment could afford to do so, but there was an exhibition of Spanish pictures in Manchester in 1857, and Whistler borrowed some money and went. Spanish painting, thereafter, was rarely entirely absent from his mind, but it existed for him rather as an idea than as an

[ 65 ]

example. It was not he, but Manet, who was to be the channel through which the influence of Spain was to affect modern painting.

Haden in the early forties had produced half a dozen plates. The arrival of his eager young brother-in-law re-kindled his enthusiasm, and in 1858 he took up the needle once more.

His first subjects were drawn from his own family—his son Arthur and his wife Dasha. He and Whistler worked in the evening, sitting side by side, as can be seen from the close similarity between Haden's "Lady Reading" and Whistler's "Reading by Lamplight." Both etchings give a vivid impression of the studious calm of the Haden household.

In the following year (1859) Whistler was apparently in London for a considerable time, and the two men went out on expeditions together. The same Greenwich Pensioner appears in both their plates in the same attitude. Afterward, Haden went up the river to Fulham and Richmond, seeking those effects of trees, rural streams, and cottages, in which he was later to excel. Whistler, characteristically enough—for he had little feeling for trees in landscape—went downstream to Wapping. His discovery of the lower Thames, however, must be left for a later chapter. He had already shown his power of etching portraits, and Mrs. Haden and her daughter Annie proved excellent models.

It has been suggested that it was the obvious superiority of his young brother-in-law in all figure subjects that decided Haden—always a shrewd judge of his own limitations as an artist—to devote himself exclusively to landscape. Painting he wisely left to those who had all day to do it in.

It was very natural, too, that Whistler, having successfully etched members of the Haden family, should attempt to paint them also. He decided to paint Mrs. Haden and her daughter together, and the result was called "At the Piano."

"At the Piano" marked a great advance in Whistler's art. Although he was hardly aware of the fact, it showed already that he was breaking away from the influence of Courbet. If any other artist's influence is to be seen it is that of Fantin, who had produced several pictures full of the quiet domestic atmosphere of his own home and marked by a curiously decorative use of the lower edges of picture frames. This device Whistler adopted and used with great effect.

"At the Piano" shows very clearly his interest in the organization of tones. It was already a "Harmony." In a softly lighted room Mrs. Haden, dressed in black, is seen in profile playing the piano. Her daughter Annie, also in profile but in a white dress, rests her elbows on the piano and listens. The background is gray, or grayish white, with green and gold bands. The carpet is red and harmonizes with the red cloth on a little table against the wall. The black of the dress is repeated in the violin case which lies on the floor under the piano, and the whole picture is bathed in a limpid atmosphere of filtered daylight, which touches softly the high lights on the polished wood of the instrument and gleams on the molding of the dull gold frames. It is the first picture by Whistler which fore-shadows his later development.

He offered the picture to the Salon of 1859. It was refused. He was not disappointed, as he was known al-ready to belong to Courbet's circle and it was almost a matter of course that his picture should be rejected. Fantin offered three of the best of his early paintings, but the jury of the Salon would admit none of them. Ribot and Legros were excluded also.

The admirable Bonvin, indignant at an obvious injus-tice, determined to organize an exhibition of his young friends' work in his own "Flemish studio" in the rue St. Jacques. He did so and induced all his friends to come and see it. Courbet himself came, and paused before Whistler's work with a gesture of admiration.

However, the admiration of Courbet was more hin-drance than help in the struggle for recognition in Paris. Whistler wondered if the authorities in England would be more sympathetic. The picture which he had sent to the Salon of 1859 he determined to offer to the Royal Academy of 1860. It was accepted, and Armstrong in his "Reminiscences" says very justly: "The virulent abuse which Whistler and his later friends delighted in pouring on the Royal Academy must appear very misplaced and absurd to those who know that his first picture, painted in an unaccustomed manner by an utterly unknown artist who was, besides, a foreigner, was hung in a very good place on the line, and was bought before the Exhibition opened by a Royal Academician, John Philip."

After the hostility of France, England must have seemed a very wonderful place to the young artist; indeed he wrote in enthusiastic terms to his friends in Paris, urging them to come over and share in the unexampled prosperity which awaited them in England.

"Come, come, come," he wrote to Fantin, "just come, come to me at once! Here you will find all you need to continue in the vein and with the abundance that has begun for you. No idea, theory or any other nonsense must prevent your coming here immediately. Incidentally, I beg of you, be advised, for once; let my lucky star influence you just a little bit. You know I have always assured you that something would come your way. Well, it is England, my dear fellow, that advances with both hands outstretched to young artists."

Legros, who was in difficulties with his father's creditors, accepted the invitation, became a naturalized British subject and lived in England for the rest of his life. Fantin visited England, but continued to live in Paris. The letter

reveals an unusually attractive side of Whistler's character, an optimism which was to receive some rude shocks
and an interest in the fortunes of others which did not long
survive.

For a time it seemed as if England could hardly do
too much for him. Sir Henry (then Mr.) Cole even let
him have a studio in the iron building at South Kensington which was ultimately to be superseded by the Victoria and Albert Museum. The history of the next few years
is the story of the gradual strengthening of his ties in England, and the gradual loosening of those which bound him
to France. His French masters, he thought, had set him on
the right track. It remained only for him to nourish his
own individual talent, and the fame and wealth which
London offered would fall into his hand.

Almost at the same time when Whistler was abandoning the thought of a permanent residence in Paris, a
dour provincial arrived in the French capital and, seeking
out his friend Zola, growled under his breath that a time
would come when a handful of apples honestly and compe-
tently painted would be enough to cause a revolution in
art. The name of the newcomer was Cézanne.

# CHAPTER III

## THE DISCOVERY OF THE THAMES

IT was in 1859 that Whistler began a series of etchings of the lower Thames, ignoring the opinion of his contemporaries that such subjects were, by their very nature, ugly and unpicturesque. The barges and warehouses, the forest of masts in the Pool, the longshore scenes, Whistler found picturesque enough. His esthetic sensibility was always in advance of his time, and in an age appalled by the horror of industrialism and seeking beauty only in the past which it had destroyed, he was one of the first to be conscious of the beauty of wharves and shipping, of the accidental silhouettes of factories, in a word, of that beauty of the modern city, which has so little in common with the dignified urbanity of the eighteenth century. Paris was already being tidied up, but London was still unspoiled, still haphazard, still magnificently unselfconscious, and nowhere more so than among the docks of the lower Thames.

He went among them first as an etcher and as a realist. He was still interested in the aspect of things, in their hard outlines and well-defined forms. He sat down patiently to draw what he saw, for the time had not yet come when he was to absorb the imaginative essence of the river and from a memory of twilight to distill in his own studio the poetry of the nocturnes. Working in the meticulous manner of the "French Set," he set down on the copper with great fidelity the varying textures of bricks and beams and rafters in the old houses by the waterside. His drawing was careful almost to excess, although he had already learned the trick of blurring outlines in the foreground to represent the impossibility of focusing the eye upon near and distant objects at the same time. Of the sketchiness of some of his later work there is hardly a trace, although in the economy of line in "Old Westminster Bridge" there is already a hint of the simplification which was to come to its logical extreme in the etchings of Venice.

Most of his subjects were found farther down the river than Westminster. The early "Thames Warehouses" is the simple treatment of a theme which is seen at its most elaborate height in the famous plate of "Black Lion Wharf," and in the etching which he somewhat perversely entitled "Thames Police," after the manner of those who paint a large landscape with one small figure on the horizon and call it "The Red Hat."

The lower river, winding through the East End of London, was difficult to reach in the days before underground railways, and Whistler, to save time, took up his quarters at a little inn near Wapping pier. Here he stayed for several months, and his friends would come down and

WHISTLER ETCHING DURING
THE TOUR TO ALSACE: *From an
impression in the Victoria and Albert
Museum.*

WHISTLER ETCHING ON THE
LOWER THAMES, 1861: *From an
impression in the Victoria and Albert
Museum.*

enliven his evenings with songs and talk. Poynter came, and Legros, and Du Maurier, when he returned from Antwerp. Even wealthy men like Ionides and Serjeant Thomas found their way to the public-house by the river. Thomas was a good friend in many ways. He admired Whistler's etchings and allowed him to print them on a press installed in his own house in Bond Street, beneath which he had opened a shop. The plates were bitten there also, while Thomas plied the young artist with excellent port. He even brought Delâtre from Paris to help and, when the work was completed, he organized an exhibition.

Whistler has left a small etching showing himself at work on the riverside with Serjeant Thomas standing behind him, both men in the high silk hats of the period. The new formality of Whistler's attire is in amusing contrast to the etching showing him at work during the Alsace tour when he still wore the straw hat with the floating ribbons.

The friendship between Whistler and Thomas did not last forever. To be Whistler's patron was an affair of infinite delicacy. The angry artist sent Thomas one of his pungent little notes, and the old man, in Whistler's somewhat unfeeling phrase, "died by return of post."

Whistler was not yet so difficult. He had great social charm, and his gaiety was as light-hearted as in Paris. He gave a dinner party to which his friends and the landlord of the inn were invited with several of the local bargees, and from the lighted windows French and English songs rang out across the mud-flats of the river, while Jimmie flirted with the landlord's wife.

His work he took very seriously, and he labored for months in order not only to etch the Thames but to paint it. The hard winter offered him an unusual opportunity, and on Christmas Day, 1860, and on two other days, he painted one of the most interesting of his early canvases—"The Thames in Ice." This and his other painting of the same period—"The Demolition of Old Westminster Bridge"—are different from anything he painted later and seem to point to quite another development of his talent from that which actually happened. Had Whistler persisted in the way which, in 1860, he seemed to have chosen, he would now be considered as one of the founders of impressionism. Instead, he is an artist who refuses to be classified, and perhaps the world is the richer for his refusal.

There is a third painting to be considered, a painting with an interest more personal, for besides being a view of shipping in the river it includes the portraits of Legros and of the red-haired woman who was to play an important part in Whistler's life.

Legros, now settled in England, was Whistler's most intimate friend. Fantin, although he had stayed in France, was on the friendliest terms with them both, and his absence led to a long correspondence from which much can be learned of Whistler's early days in London. Fantin's replies are lost—Whistler collected neither other people's letters nor other people's work—but Whistler's epistles remain, evidence of the warmth of his nature and his absorbed interest in the yet difficult art of painting. In them, too, we find the first mention of Jo. In a most important letter [1] he speaks of his efforts to paint the Thames from a first-floor balcony with figures in the foreground. One of these figures was Legros, one was a boatman, and another was a girl—"horribly difficult to paint." Her head gave him a great deal of trouble; he painted it three times and was afraid to do any more for fear of losing freshness. Her head fascinated him. "Ah! but let me describe the head to you: it has the loveliest hair you ever have seen! a coppered, not a gilded, red—a perfect Venetian dream! a skin whitish yellow, or gilded, if you prefer."

Toward the end of the letter he uses about her what Bénédite calls *un mot un peu vif,* from which we may conclude that she was not yet his mistress, since such words are more likely to be employed immediately before than immediately after such a conquest. However, she was soon to become so, and she lived with Whistler for about ten years.

Her real name was Joanna Heffernan, and she was the daughter of a bohemian Irishman, who accepted the situation readily enough, and always referred to Whistler

[1] Quoted by L. Bénédite, Gazette des Beaux-Arts, XXXIII (1905), p. 496.

as "me son-in-law." She was young and well made, and her face, although melancholy, was attractive. But the most striking thing about her was her hair, and, as we have seen from the letter to Fantin, it was this which first attracted Whistler. Red hair had a fascination for him throughout his life, although whether Jo inspired this preference or merely benefited by it we do not know.

At first their relations were the casual ones of artist and model, but Whistler soon began to desire a less interrupted intimacy. In spite of the storms which had brought to an end his first experiment of keeping house with a woman, he was quite ready to try again. He might well have hesitated with another "Fumette," romantic and temperamental; but Jo was different. We hear nothing even of the quick temper of her race, and her presence was one more inducement to Whistler to give up his wanderings and settle permanently in London.

However, although Jo had become a necessary part of Whistler's existence, he did not end his wanderings yet, but took her with him on his travels. After his long labor at Wapping, Whistler felt he deserved a holiday, and in the summer of 1861 he carried Jo off to Brittany.

The choice of place was itself a tribute to the influence of Courbet, for it was the realist who had discovered the wild beauty of the Breton coast; and the pictures Whistler painted there point to the same conclusion.

Whistler, in later life, strongly resented the suggestion

that he had been influenced by Courbet, and indeed the "Whistler manner" is the repudiation of all the great realist stood for. But in the early sixties, and as late as 1865, Courbet was undoubtedly his master, whether Whistler thought of him as such or not. That Courbet regarded Whistler as one of his pupils may be seen from a letter which he wrote to his father from Trouville, in 1865:

> I have done thirty-five canvases, which has dumfounded everyone. . . . I have taken eighty sea-baths. Six days ago we were still bathing with the painter Whistler, who is here with me; he is an Englishman who is a pupil of mine.

Even supposing that Courbet, who was not a modest man, exaggerated his own influence on others, one has only to compare some of Whistler's most important early paintings in order to realize how much he owed to the older man. Whistler's "L'Homme à la Pipe," is very similar in design to Courbet's self-portrait *à la pipe*. Both Courbet and Whistler painted portraits of themselves "in a big hat," and if this is mere accident, the similarity of Courbet's "Wave" and Whistler's "Blue Wave" cannot be dismissed.

In the winter of 1861, Whistler took Jo to Paris, and they lived together in the Boulevard des Batignolles. It was then, according to Pennell's account, that Courbet visited them and that Whistler made Jo take down her magnificent hair for the master's admiration. Courbet was moved to paint the beautiful picture which he called "La Belle Irlandaise," and which is reproduced in the present volume.[2]

Whether Whistler's "Blue Wave" was painted in 1862 or not, in the previous year he painted "Alone with the Tide," which shows the influence of Courbet plainly enough. Yet in the winter following, when he was living in Paris, he was able to plan and carry out a painting which owes nothing to Courbet at all.

Whistler had a new idea for a picture, an idea as yet only half formulated. Somewhere or other he had seen Théophile Gautier's poem "Symphonie en blanc majeur," and as he watched Jo moving about the studio in her white dress he had a new conception of what painting could be. He would paint her in white, and everything about her

[2] The whole question of the dates in the Courbet-Whistler connection is inextricably confused. Whistler's "Blue Wave" is dated 1862, while Courbet's "Wave" was not *exhibited* until the Salon of 1870. But the first recorded exhibition of Whistler's picture was not until 1892, when it was shown at the Goupil Gallery. Pennell thought that Courbet's painting was inspired by Whistler's, but the evidence is inconclusive, and the conclusion itself excessively unlikely. There is a similar obscurity regarding the portrait of Jo. Georges Riat in his "Gustave Courbet" (Paris, 1906), p. 228, speaking of Jo, says:
"She was the mistress of Whistler, with whom she lived five years, and to whom she bore a son. Courbet has painted her as a bust, a left profile, her throat hidden by a white scarf; in her left hand she holds a mirror in which she is admiring her magnificently clear, ruddy, complexion, while with her right she lifts up her opulent tresses of hair. This splendid portrait is dated Trouville, 1866. The letter, mentioned above, might suggest that it was begun in 1865, and completed the following year. There is in existence a copy, slightly different."

[ 78 ]

LA BELLE IRLANDAISE *(Jo): By Gustave Courbet. Photograph from Messrs. Alexander Reid and Lefevre, Ltd.*

should be white also. All the furniture was removed from one end of the studio, and the walls were hung with white cloth. Jo, in a long white dress, was posed on a whitish rug. Whistler set to work and for months struggled with his new problem. For this painting was not to be a transcript from nature; it was not to be a portrait full of the individuality of the sitter; still less was it to tell a story, or be a subject picture in the accepted sense of the word. But if it had no subject, it was to have a theme, just as a piece of music might. It was the first germ of the literary-musical idea which was later to become almost an obsession with him.

At last the picture was almost finished, and the artist found himself at the end of his strength. It is thought that he poisoned himself with the quantities of white lead necessary for the work, but whatever the cause, he left Paris for the South. His intention was to go to Madrid, and in order to recover his health on the way he stopped, with Jo, at Guéthary, between Biarritz and St.-Jean-de-Luz.

Nothing is more curious at this point than the object of Whistler's journey. Having finished "The White Girl," he abandoned for the moment all thought of further progress on the same lines and turned once more to Velasquez.

Whistler was full of enthusiasm for his pilgrimage. He wrote to Fantin urging him to join them, and as he could not, promised him a complete account of "The Surrender of Breda," and all the chief pictures in the Prado. But

Whistler was never to reach Madrid. He stayed on at Guéthary, bathing and lying in the sun. He painted very little, and when he did make up his mind to cross the Spanish frontier, got no farther than Fuenterrabía.

It seems strange that he should turn back when he had gone so far, strange that the dream of so many artists of his generation should remain for him unfulfilled, when so little additional effort would have made dreaming reality. Yet sometimes a place, a country, or one particular picture, is a greater influence when not seen. From his admiration for Velasquez he retained throughout his life something which was an inspiration to him, although it is very hard to say what it is. His later paintings had an elegance and a darkness of tone which seems to bring them near to those of the Spanish master. Whistler thought so himself, and his first biographer, Théodore Duret, thought it necessary to devote a whole chapter to establishing their relationship, and clearing Whistler of the charge of being unduly influenced.

The reason for his return, his purpose unaccomplished, may have been the condition of Jo's health. She seemed to have been delicate—one can judge as much from his paintings of her—but not dangerously so. In fact she survived him. But she may well have wearied of the eternal coming and going. All her life had been unsettled, first with a dissipated father, then as an artist's model, then as Whistler's mistress, model, and traveling companion combined.

[ 80 ]

She longed for a settled home, and, as she knew no French, preferred to live in London. Whistler for some time had been cherishing a similar hope of more tranquil existence, but he had not yet made up his mind where to settle. Sloane Street and its neighborhood was very well for respectable and comparatively wealthy surgeons like his brother-in-law, but was not very suitable for impecunious artists living with women they had not troubled to marry. Wapping was both too uncomfortable and too remote for long residence.

During the last few years he had been a good deal in London and, unable to paint at his brother-in-law's house (although he certainly etched there), he had taken a studio in Bloomsbury, which then, as now, was a kind of second artistic colony in London. It was full of roomy eighteenth-century town houses with high, well-proportioned windows and lofty ceilings. Sky-lights were rare, but Whistler never cared for them, indeed in his later days developed a positive dislike of anything but the light from an ordinary window. Whistler was influenced by their dingy dignity, and as he had still very little money, the cheapness of the rooms was an additional inducement.

His studio was a single chamber large enough to have one corner curtained off to serve as a bedroom, although, according to Armstrong, the curtain was more of a symbol than a protection, for it consisted of nothing but a minute square of threadbare brocade augmented, when need arose,

[ 81 ]

by a towel hung over a clothes-line. Whistler was used to primitive conditions in Paris, and was quite at home. When he was not using the studio himself he let it to Du Maurier, still his close friend, but was forever bustling in to interrupt his work with inquiry and laughter. William De Morgan, the novelist, has left an engaging account of the noises which proceeded from the room Whistler had taken.

> In 1860 or '61 I occupied a first-floor front studio in Newman Street. There I pretended to be a Painter. The back room was the den of a young artist who sang French songs all day. It was not, I believe, his own studio, but a friend's. When this friend turned up, as he generally did, the noise and laughter, the lulls for comic anecdotes and the outbursts that followed, the suggestions of capsized furniture and chases round the room—well! they were what I have heard described as a *caution!* When the actual occupant was alone, he made no more noise than went with the singing of an enjoyable selection of French songs; I think the "Sieur de Framboisy" was a favorite. The young man in possession was Du Maurier, and the visiting landlord was Whistler.[3]

Du Maurier was beginning to make a little money as an illustrator. He illustrated long serial stories for the Leisure Hour and similar periodicals, for it was the hey-

[3] Thomas Armstrong, C.B., "A Memoir" (London, 1912).

[ 82 ]

day of reproductive wood-engraving and the beginning of "the sixties," the great period of English illustration. Most young artists of the time worked for the magazines, and Whistler was no exception. He contributed two illustrations to Good Words and four to Once a Week. The latter periodical contains among its list of illustrators, in the volume for 1862, the names of Du Maurier, H. K. Browne, Charles Keene, M. J. Lawless, Millais, Poynter, Sandys, Simeon Solomon, Fred Walker, and Whistler—a notable gathering of afterwards famous artists.

One cannot help feeling when turning over the pages of these old journals that half the honor of their illustrations should go to the engravers. The designers gave them little help, for none of them accommodated his style to the requirements of wood-engraving, Whistler least of all. His drawing for "The Relief Fund in Lancashire" is a maze of spidery and entangled lines which only the infinite patience and dexterity of Swain or some equally competent engraver could have reproduced in facsimile.[4] His two illustrations to poems in the same volume show more understanding of the requirements of book illustration. Jo seems to have been his model for all these.

Du Maurier's ambition was to appear in Punch, but he was compelled to design many initial letters for its pages before he received a commission for a drawing. The first drawing accepted is of great interest and is here re-

[4] Once a Week, 1862, p. 140.

produced because it contains a caricature of Whistler going with Du Maurier to a photographer's and being reprimanded for smoking. "Please to remember, gentlemen, that this is not a common Hartist's studio."

Whistler came into touch not only with the good engravers but with the English etchers. In the library of the Victoria and Albert Museum is deposited a manuscript volume of the Minutes of the Junior Etching Club, a body much less known and more short-lived than the "Old" Etching Club of which Haden was for a time a member. The Junior Club was founded in 1857, and Charles Keene was among its earliest supporters. Millais joined later, while Rossetti and Ford Madox Brown were both invited, but declined to belong.

The fame of Whistler's Paris etchings made him an obvious candidate for membership, and at a general meeting held on Wednesday, July 6, 1859, he was proposed, and in November unanimously elected. However, he seems to have been conscious from the first that the Junior Etching Club provided no very sympathetic background for his own talents. Its members regarded etching as a method of illustration, a conception against which Whistler was perpetually in revolt. He was asked to contribute a plate on the subject of "Black-eyed Susan" to a "Collection of National and Patriotic Songs," but he could never bring himself to do it, and the prospect was abandoned. He very rarely attended the meetings and might never have con-

[ 84 ]

tributed to any of the club's publications, but for the fact that the death of one of the members left room for two plates in a collection of "Miscellaneous Etchings," and Whistler consented to supply the two etchings required. The club was dissolved in 1864, and its publications are now chiefly remembered for Whistler's contributions.

Both Whistler and Du Maurier were famous for their songs, and were acceptable entertainers long before they were celebrated as artists. They soon penetrated into the more cultivated stratum of London society, or rather into that rich foreign fraction of it which is so often the first in England to welcome a youth of talent. It does not seem that Haden opened many social doors for his young brother-in-law. Perhaps those he did open presented too dull a prospect for Whistler's taste. The first stranger's house which welcomed him was that of a foreigner.

Alec Ionides was now in London, and when "At the Piano" had a success at the Academy, Ionides sought him out. His father, Alexander Ionides, one of a group of wealthy Greek merchants, had a large house on Tulse Hill, and Whistler spent almost every Sunday evening there. The Ionides family had none of the stiffness of their English counterparts. Their home was always full of artists, poets, and musicians, and they had a passion for charades, impromptu dramatic entertainments, and sing-songs of every kind.

The two friends, Whistler and Du Maurier, threw

[ 85 ]

themselves into these entertainments with the zest of schoolboys, and their repertoire of amusing songs gathered from the *cafés chantants* of Paris made them great favorites.

Du Maurier would sing in French:

> "Fie! on these cheap wines of Spain,
> They were not meant for us,
> 'Tis a wine costing only four sous
> That we drink in place of champagne."

or—

> "While coming back from Barbizon
> Zon zon zainé zon zon,
> I chanced to meet Mam'selle Suzon.
> Zon zon zainé zon zon."

while Whistler, seizing an umbrella and using it as a banjo, would chant one of the Negro ballads which have since become so familiar:

> "Swing low, sweet chariot,
> Comin' for to carry me home."

Such a house as that of Ionides can be of very great use to a young artist. He becomes known in a short time to a surprising number of people, especially if some eccentricity of dress or behavior makes him easy to remember. It is in everybody's interest to emphasize the talents of an artist acquaintance, especially to those who do not know him, and his chances of having his early works favorably received are very much increased by a little social notoriety.

Whistler was peculiarly suited to profit by such opportunities, for his eye-glass, his swarthy complexion, his mop of black hair, and, in summer, his suit of white duck made him conspicuous everywhere.

Luke Ionides, a member of the hospitable family, gave Whistler his first commission for a portrait and came to the Newman Street studio to sit. Whistler painted him in the manner which he had learned from Courbet, that is to say, with heavy impasto and with considerable emphasis on light and shade. He had not yet begun to "arrange" his sitters into a simple silhouette against a purely decorative background. The Whistlerian "manner" was still unthought of, and the Ionides picture was painted in the same fashion as that of "La Mère Gérard" or the old man smoking a pipe, or the early portrait of himself. Whistler was still experimenting.

He was still in close touch with the Hadens. The attractions of the Newman Street studio and of Jo (wherever she lived) may have taken him out at nights, but he must have passed a considerable part of the day amid the respectable dignity of his sister's house in Sloane Street, for in the same year in which he painted the portrait of Luke Ionides he was also at work on his second painting of the Haden household, the canvas which was to be known as "The Music Room." Later when he began to make his musical titles retrospective he renamed it "Harmony in Green and Rose." M. Bénédite, by measuring the length of Annie

[ 87 ]

Haden's skirts and calculating how much she had grown since she figured in "At the Piano," sought to prove that "The Music Room" must have been painted several years later, and that Whistler had already been influenced by the example of Japanese art.[5] He admits however that there is no trace of English influence in the painting, and it seems safer to regard it as one of those sudden forward strides which young artists sometimes make surprisingly early in their career.

For "The Music Room" is a singularly beautiful and interesting painting, and must have exercised all Whistler's skill. He was afterwards to simplify his problems by decreasing the depth, limiting himself to a single figure and lighting that figure *en face*. In "The Music Room" he does just the opposite, seeming to seek difficulties in order to overcome them. There are three figures, although one—that of Mrs. Haden—is seen only in the mirror which runs at an acute angle up the left-hand side of the composition. Beyond the mirror is an unseen open window through which streams the light illuminating the edges of the flowered curtains that conceal it from view. In the light of the window sits Annie Haden, reading, in white, while sharply silhouetted against the edge of her dress and against the light wall is a tall woman in a black riding habit and the small pill-box hat of the early sixties, who seems to be walking out of the picture.

[5] See Gazette des Beaux-Arts, XXXIII (1905), p. 506.

ANNIE HADEN: *From an impression
in the Victoria and Albert Museum.*

MISS ALEXANDER: *In the possession of Mrs. Spring-Rice.*

The whole composition is extremely daring in its asymmetrical complexity, and only a miracle of tact holds it together. It is a *tour de force* for a young artist, and in spite of its cleverness the canvas does succeed in conveying an impression of singular charm, and makes us regret that Whistler in his later efforts to simplify his backgrounds should have deprived us of many glimpses into such tranquil interiors, sympathetically seen and beautifully painted.

Annie Haden was a great favorite with Whistler, and he with her. She was very patient in sitting for him, and he immortalized her girlish grace not only in "The Music Room" and "At the Piano," but in the famous etching on which he declared he would be willing to rest his reputation. It is an exquisite plate, firmly and solidly constructed and informed by the most delicate understanding. The dainty figure of the young girl, in her full skirt and little round hat, is a perpetual tribute to his insight into feminine character, the exuberance of childhood just melting into the melancholy of adolescence. "Annie Haden" is one of the great portrait etchings of the world.

But Whistler's devotion to his half-sister and her daughter could not outweigh his growing dislike of Seymour Haden. The surgeon was a man of determined, not to say violent, character. He had always thought of Whistler as a boy and he resented his growing independence. He reserved the right to criticize his brother-in-law's productions, and this Whistler would not stand from one whom he

[ 89 ]

regarded as an amateur. We must not forget that Haden's fame as an etcher was still in the future. Haden had proved a useful patron up to a point. He had bought Fantin's copy of "The Marriage at Cana," he had bought Whistler's picture of "The Thames in Ice" and he bought a painting by Legros. But he could not resist the temptation of tampering with his juniors' work. The perspective of Legros's picture bothered him. He did not think it was right and, as the painting was his own property, he altered it to suit his own opinions. Not long afterwards Legros was in London and, calling on Haden, was delighted to see his work, for the first time, hung in an expensive frame. Soon, however, he realized what had been done. Whistler's help was demanded, and the two young men carried off the picture to the Newman Street studio, where Legros removed Haden's work with turpentine. The angry patron followed hot-foot, but when he arrived and found the picture restored to its original condition he could only take it back again with as good a grace as possible, which (as he was Haden) was not much. It is not surprising that Legros's gratitude and Whistler's friendliness were tempered by such an occurrence.

Whistler, moreover, had now no need of his brother-in-law. He had plenty of friends, and in the early sixties was not the isolated figure he was afterwards to become. He might be in revolt against the "anecdotage" of most English painting, but he was still in close touch with the young English artists he had known in Paris. He painted still life in Poynter's studio in Grafton Street, and was still on terms of intimacy with Armstrong. The latter describes how a party of young artists visited the Ionides household, and the occasion was fraught with such consequences that the passage must be quoted in full.

> Rossetti's first appearance at the Tulse Hill house was on one summer Sunday, when a cab-load, such a cab-load as was perhaps never seen except at an Irish funeral, set out from Chelsea: Whistler, Rossetti, Du Maurier, Legros, Ridley, and myself were in or on it. It seems to me that there were others in that four-wheeler, Poynter perhaps, but I am not sure, and I want to be accurate. The occasion was a memorable one. Then for the first time was revealed to this artistic circle the beauty of two girls, relations or connections of the Ionides family, and daughters of the Consul-General for Greece in London, Mr. Spartali. We were all *à genoux* before them and, of course, burned with a desire to try and paint them.[6]

Whistler was immensely attracted at least by the pictorial qualities of Miss Spartali. She represented a new type to him, different alike from the women he had known in Paris and from Jo. She had a slenderness and an elegance which he could already appreciate. Her face was at once spiritual and voluptuous. He heard the people round him

[6] Thomas Armstrong, C.B., "A Memoir" (London, 1912), p. 195.

[ 91 ]

60168

say that she was a "Rossetti type." There, too, was Rossetti himself, a man as much talked of in London as Courbet had been in Paris. What a strange figure, with his square beard, his massive projecting forehead, and his voluminous, ill-fitting clothes!

Whistler looked at him with a certain envy, for he was already a legend. He was acknowledged as a master and had disciples who worshiped him. He was poet as well as painter, and the high priest of a strange esthetic cult. His life, too, was mysterious and tragic. He had loved a shop-girl, a pale ghost who had been the inspiration of his finest work. He had married her, but she died almost at once. Some said that she poisoned herself in grief at his infidelities, and that it was in a fit of remorse that he flung the manuscript of his poems into her open grave. Yet in the cab he had been high-spirited, almost childish. A strange man! Whistler determined to know him better.

## CHAPTER IV

### ROSSETTI AND THE INFLUENCE OF JAPAN

IN England toward the middle of the nineteenth century there could be seen the same opposition between academic and rebel art, as in contemporary France. The conditions, however, were not the same. The degenerate eclecticism of the English Academy was compounded of different elements from that of equivalent bodies in France. But between academic painters of all nations there is in any given age a certain similarity. The real difference was between the French and English rebels. In France, as we have seen, the cry of those in revolt against official art was the cry of naturalism. In England the promising young men belonged to the group loosely and somewhat inaccurately known as the Pre-Raphaelite Brotherhood. In its early days the dominant personality had been Hunt, but by the time that Whistler came to England the young man who absorbed most of the attention which the public had to spare for esthetic matters was undoubtedly Dante Gabriel Rossetti.

It was typical of the difference between the two nations that the French sought to return to the starkness and primitiveness of peasant life, while the English, in closer touch with the horrors of industrialism, and for that reason more depressed by it, strove to renounce the age altogether, and to return to a happier epoch, an imagined Golden Era, compounded of the atmosphere of the Middle Ages and of the early Italian Renaissance. Romanticism is both Hydra and Proteus, and the complicated web of Pre-Raphaelitism is too thick to be unraveled in a paragraph. The most apparently incongruous elements had gone to its making. Malory and Melozzo da Forli, Horace Walpole and Walter Scott, the Florentine Primitives and the German Nazarenes, the "Génie du Christianisme" and "Tracts for the Times." It was at once a protest against factories and a yearning for the altars of the Catholic Church, a search for simplicity and the apotheosis of bric-à-brac, a dream of impossible medievalism and a pedantic determination to paint the natural appearance of things in all their detail.

Its aims were as confused as its origins. The cry of Hunt was the old one of "back to Nature," although by that he seems to have meant truth of local color at the cost of general effect and truth of atmosphere. "Back to Nature" in France meant back to life as it is lived. In England the cry meant back to life as it might have been lived in ancient times. But these ancient times were conceived in picturesque terms by artists to whom history was not a plain record, but an excuse for dreaming. Truth put on a costume of masquerade, and the master of ceremonies decided, quite arbitrarily, that the fancy dress ball should be "Period Early Florentine." In matters of detail "truth" meant pretending to see the flowers in a distant trellis as clearly as those in the foreground and painting them in as vivid colors.

There was no really valid reason why Raphael should have been made the scapegoat of the Brotherhood. It was not admiration for the Urbinese which made English painting bankrupt; it was a withering at the roots due, in part at least, to the rapid change from an agricultural to an industrial civilization. The lesson of Hogarth had been forgotten, the achievement of Turner misunderstood, the example of Constable ignored. What remained was a degenerate eclecticism. Raphael undoubtedly was among its ancestors, but that was no fault of his.

It is unnecessary to labor the point that without Rossetti there would have been no Pre-Raphaelite Brotherhood at all. Rossetti *was* the Brotherhood, however much he may have been influenced by others, however negligible as a painter he may have been when the movement was inaugurated. Its exotic emotionalism was entirely his, the strain of highly colored poetry which was imported into it was his doing, for he was primarily a poet and for him a picture was not an arrangement of form and color, but the reflection of a state of mind.

We are in no danger in these days of overvaluing such an achievement as his. Rather are we excessively Puritan in our attitude to pictorial art, and inclined to the belief that a richly stored mind is a positive disadvantage to a painter.

To a public accustomed to academic insipidities Rossetti offered nothing that was different in kind from the paintings against which he was in revolt. He still looked upon art as a vessel for conveying the wine of poetical emotion. His potation was better, richer, more profoundly impregnated with the complicated bouquet of European culture, but the principle involved was the same. It was the same gesture. Like the academicians he did not cry, "Look!" but, "Drink!" The public drank and did not like it. They preferred the home-brew until they had learned to appreciate the Rossetti flavor. The Pre-Raphaelite revolution dwindled into a mere question of taste, and that not in the larger meaning of the word, but taste as it is understood in kitchens and at dinner tables. The refinement of the palate effected by Rossetti and his friends had nothing to do with art.

In both England and France the new movements provoked a great deal of hostility even from those who might have been supposed more sensitive than their fellows, but the path of the English rebels was smoothed by what must have seemed to them an unexpected and Heaven-sent blessing. Ruskin's defense of Turner had already made his reputation as an art critic and he was rapidly advancing to a position of almost papal infallibility. He took up his pen in strong support of the Pre-Raphaelite Brotherhood, and did as much as any one man could do, if not in making them popular, at least in giving them respectable status.

The Pre-Raphaelite Brotherhood had been founded in 1854, the year before Whistler went to Paris. When Whistler came to England, Rossetti occupied a peculiarly commanding position. He was known both as poet and as painter, and his circle of admirers, though comparatively small, was fanatically devoted. The young men of the newer generation such as Burne-Jones and Morris looked upon him as a master, and he had already painted some of his most famous pictures. Yet he himself was desperately unhappy.

Rightly or wrongly, Rossetti regarded himself as partly responsible for the overdose of laudanum which put an end to the pathetic career of Elizabeth Siddal, and at first his grief was so intense that he was hardly sane. His family, whose members were devoted to him, saw that he did not do himself injury during these terrible days. He lived with them for a time, and then moved into chambers in Lincoln's Inn Fields.

Whistler was in London, and it was inevitable that Rossetti and he should meet sooner or later, even if the Ionides household had not provided a rendezvous. They seem to have enjoyed one another's company in spite of the differences in their aims and outlook. Whistler—he was still a man who thought of friendship as one of the most precious things in life—liked Rossetti, and referred to him much later, when his own artistic sympathies had flowed wider and wider apart from those of the Pre-Raphaelite Brotherhood, as "no painter, you know, but a poet and a gentleman."

Gradually, to all outward appearance at least, Rossetti recovered from the shock of his wife's death, and began to look about for a comfortable house where he might paint his pictures and entertain his friends. Chelsea, at that time, was a semirural district, with no Embankment and no very easy access to other parts of London.

Charles II had found it a convenient place in which to keep Nell Gwyn, and throughout the eighteenth century it had been a favorite residence for the mistresses of the nobility. The waters of the Thames were yet unsullied, and on the opposite side of the river were unspoiled woods where Addison had heard the nightingale. Boat-builders' jetties added a picturesque touch to the sandy shore, and the river itself was pleasantly animated, for Londoners had not yet forgotten the pleasures of traveling by water. Vauxhall Gardens, a little farther to the east than what has since become the most famous part of Chelsea, enlivened the distance with fireworks and air balloons.

By the beginning of the nineteenth century, artists had already begun to discover its rural charm. Maclise lived at No. 4 Cheyne Walk for some years and was succeeded by Dyce, who died there. In the same house George Eliot was to die some years later. At the end of what was then called Lindsey Row, there stood an old public-house with the engaging name of the Aquatic Stores. Next door to the inn was a tumbledown house with green palings, and to this house came one evening an eccentric old gentleman who demanded lodging. On being asked his name, he asked the landlady's in return. She replied, "Booth," and her visitor remarked that Booth was as good a name as another and that he proposed to adopt it. He became known as "Admiral Booth" for no particular reason, and spent many hours at the place, gazing up the river toward the west. He had a passion for sunsets, especially when in autumn they grew red and flamboyant. Perhaps his use of a telescope earned for him his naval title, but his neighbors seem never to have pierced the mystery of his identity so long as he stayed there. In December, 1851, he was taken ill in the house with green palings, and on the 19th he died. The connoisseur of sunsets was J. M. W. Turner.

It is interesting to reflect that Whistler, coming after him, stood almost upon the same spot, and, too late, as it were, for the sunset, became the interpreter of the hour which followed, when a still luminous twilight lay upon the river and when the factory chimneys which had sprung up the other bank were transformed into minarets and campaniles. The same magic was to enthrall them both.

In the early sixties Chelsea's most famous inhabitant was Carlyle, who found it a convenient retreat from which to denounce the neighboring city. Rossetti, too, wished to be away from the town, and he discovered a house fronting the river that, in spite of its great size, seemed suitable for his purpose. This was No. 16 Cheyne Walk, then called Queen's House, but subsequently known as Tudor House, both names springing from the legend that Queen Elizabeth had lived there as a child. Certainly a Tudor mansion had stood on the same spot, and the wild garden, in which Rossetti kept so many strange beasts, had been part of the park, but the house itself was rebuilt in the time of Wren, whether by his own hand or not is disputed. It is a handsome edifice with large and stately rooms, and Rossetti was attracted by the conveniences it offered both for painting and for entertaining his friends. He moved in during October, 1862. Whistler, fired by his example, took rooms in Queen's Road, now called Royal Hospital Road, and shortly afterwards removed to his first house in Lindsey Row.

Lindsey Row was the continuation of Cheyne Walk to the west beyond Battersea Bridge, then a curious wooden structure built upon piles driven into the mud. It took its name from Lindsey House, once occupied by Robert, Earl of Lindsey. In the nineteenth century the mansion was divided into five, and it was in one of these apartments that Whistler chose to live.

Eastward from Whistler's house stretched the old river-front of Chelsea. The Embankment was as yet unthought of, and a multitude of boatmen's jetties stretched from the tree-shaded banks out over the mud-flats uncovered at low tide. Boat-builders' shanties lent the shore a charming irregularity of outline; while behind the trees, in dignified aloofness, stood the noble seventeenth- and eighteenth-century houses with extensive gardens behind and dignified iron gates before. Rossetti's house was the finest of all, with the whole of the first floor front occupied by one enormous room, fit dining-room for a peri-wigged seigneur.

It was much too big for Rossetti, or rather would have been had he not determined from the first to occupy only a small portion of the house, and to let the rest to his friends. Whistler was asked to dinner soon after his arrival, and found the inhabitants assembled. First of course was Dante Gabriel Rossetti himself. His brother William Michael Rossetti had taken a room in the house although he occupied it for a few months only. With them was Swinburne, and the young and self-conscious Meredith.

It was soon evident that the harmony of the household had already been broken. Meredith and Rossetti had had some difference; Meredith had been so indiscreet as to relate the affair to a cabman, and this indiscretion Rossetti had discovered. Across the dinner table he denounced his guest's ungentlemanly behavior, throwing his spoon into his soup with such violence that the hot liquid spurted into

[ 101 ]

Whistler's eye. Meredith's friendship and his tenancy of a room at Queen's House came to an abrupt end together.[1]

Rossetti liked Whistler, as almost everybody did at this time in his life, and Whistler appreciated the shifting crowd that gathered at Queen's House. Browning came, and Frederick Sandys, Burne-Jones and William Morris, Bell Scott and George Augustus Sala, wittiest and most enterprising of contemporary journalists.

But while other men drifted in and out, Whistler, by his near neighborhood, was a more constant visitor. Three minutes' stroll from his own door the hospitable gate of Queen's House stood open. Rossetti never worked in the evening. He sat at his ease, talking or making comic verses, and was always glad of a friendly face, for William, his brother, was of a studious disposition and joined in the household amusements only under protest. For a short time Rossetti and Whistler were very intimate, and the vexed question of influences must inevitably arise. Such influences could not be very great on either side. However friendly they might be, the background of their minds was completely different. While Rossetti dreamed of the streets

---

[1] It is only fair to add that Meredith's own story is somewhat different. According to his verbal account reported toward the end of his life, he went to call upon Rossetti one morning to arrange his proposed tenancy, and as the painter was not yet out of bed, was left to watch five eggs slowly "bleeding to death" upon five rashers of bacon. At last Rossetti appeared in a dressing-gown and swallowed the congealed mass with the air of an ogre devouring human flesh. This sight so disturbed the fastidious Meredith that he gave up all idea of living with Rossetti.

of fifteenth-century Florence, Whistler thought of the Paris boulevards, and while Rossetti's imagination was afire with the images of Italian poetry, Whistler's eyes wandered through the tall windows to where the blue mists were already creeping along the surface of the Thames. One sought a fuller life in poetry, and the other found his poetry in contemporary life.

As a painter, Rossetti's manner was already fixed; he was unlikely to be influenced by such fragments of the new French doctrine as Whistler might be able to bring before him. Had Whistler never met Courbet or Fantin, Rossetti might have influenced him profoundly, but, fortunately enough, it was too late. His admirations were firmly fixed in France.

Yet some critics have seen in "The White Girl" more than a hint of Rossetti's influence, or at least of that of the Pre-Raphaelites, for Whistler had still a certain admiration for the early work of Millais.

We find him writing to Fantin from Guéthary early in 1862, saying that he intended to return immediately to London in order to finish "The White Girl" for the Salon. He offered it to the Academy, but although two other pictures were accepted this one was not. A new gallery in Berners Street opened its doors to him, and the painting was exhibited there to the great astonishment of the public, who thought it an unsuccessful attempt to illustrate the popular novel of the day—Wilkie Collins's "The

Woman in White." This opinion, fantastic as it was, illustrates only too clearly the general notion of what pictures should be, even among those who professed to care for painting. Whistler wrote to the papers to repudiate all connection with anecdote. "My painting represents a girl dressed in white standing in front of a white curtain."

When the picture was returned to him Whistler rolled it up and carried it himself to Paris in order that it might be framed in Fantin's studio and submitted to the jury of the Salon. He had by no means lost touch with his French friends, and his growing desire to settle permanently in London did not blind him to the immense value of success in Paris. His etchings had been shown at the gallery of a dealer named Martinet, and Whistler made arrangements for "The White Girl" to be exhibited there too, in case, as he fully expected, it should be rejected from the Salon. It *was* rejected, but he had no need to fall back on the services of a dealer, for an unexpected piece of good fortune afforded "The White Girl" even more publicity than he had hoped for.

The conservative painters, who decided who should and who should not exhibit in the Salon, were growing ever more alarmed at the tendencies of the realists, a group of young men who, like their master Courbet, were not only unconventional painters, but potential revolutionaries in politics also. In 1859 some of the most promising of the younger men had been shut out. In 1863 it was determined to make the policy of exclusion even more drastic.

[ 104 ]

R. 9. TRIAL

A LADY READING (*Mrs. Seymour Haden*): *By Francis Seymour Haden. From an impression in the British Museum.*

READING BY LAMPLIGHT (*Mrs.
Seymour Haden*): *From an impression
in the Victoria and Albert Museum.*

The authorities overreached themselves. Moderate opinion demanded, with some show of reason, what purpose was served by a Salon which debarred from its walls Bracquemond, Cals, Cazin, Fantin-Latour, Harpignies, Jongkind, J. P. Laurens, Legros, Manet, Pissarro, and Whistler. Such a list of proscriptions seems fantastic today, but even in 1863, when these artists were all young men, it was manifestly absurd. There was a public outcry against such obvious injustice, and arrangements were made to exhibit the rejected works at a private gallery. The emperor made one of his most graceful gestures. He offered space in the Palais de l'Industrie, the very building in which the official Salon was held, for a *Salon des Refusés*.

It was the custom some years ago for the editor of classical texts for school use to expunge from their pages all those lines which were considered unsuitable for the eyes of adolescents. In the interests of scholarship, however, the censored passages were gathered together and included in an appendix, thus saving the inquisitive schoolboy the dreary task of reading through the whole work. The Salon of 1863 was, owing to Napoleon's benevolent interference, in somewhat similar case. The jaded or hurried visitor had no need to walk through the whole exhibition; he could go straight to the *Salon des Refusés,* which is exactly what he did. The pictures that had been rejected were all the more powerful in their effect by being gathered together in one room, instead of being scattered and lost amid the crowds of less revolutionary canvases.

[ 105 ]

Whistler plunged into the affair with zest. The atmosphere of intrigue which gathered about the emperor's action delighted him. He was horrified at the thought that his picture might, by some mistake, be exhibited at a private gallery instead of with his fellow rebels'. He had given Fantin a note to Martinet, and he now wrote to the former, urging him to destroy it lest some misfortune happen. It would be too distressing to miss his part of the grand *succès de scandale.*

Such a success the *Salon des Refusés* certainly was, but two pictures absorbed most of the attention of the visitors. A crowd stood round each of them all day, excited, gesticulating. One of the pictures was Manet's "Déjeuner sur l'herbe," with its nude figure daringly placed in the middle of a group of artists in modern conventional attire; the other was Whistler's "White Girl." It is just understandable why Manet's canvas excited so much interest and not a little hostility. There was perhaps an element of impropriety in its subject. But why should Whistler's blameless symphony have provoked so much excitement? The newspaper criticisms were, on the whole, extremely favorable, some of them absurdly so. The critics, like their comrades in England, insisted on searching for a literary meaning in the canvas, or at least for something poetical, something symbolic. To one "The White Girl" was an evoked spirit; to another, a vision. Castagnary, the defender of the realists, surprised artists and public alike by seeing in the picture: "The bride on the following day—that troubling moment when a young woman questions herself and is surprised at no longer recognizing herself as the virgin of the day before." Whistler, who had very little patience with the rhapsodies of literary men, must have been filled with an unholy joy. But, however absurd the criticisms, there could be no doubt of his success. Whistler was, for a moment, the most talked-of painter in Paris.

Another event of some importance took place in 1863: the death of Delacroix. Strange though it seems, Fantin and his friends, who looked upon Courbet as their father in art, reverenced Delacroix as their grandfather. Even his so-called romanticism was nearer to realism than the insipidities of the fashionable painters; and realism, as we have seen, was a misnomer, anyway. Fantin, at least, was a concealed romantic, in spite of the silk hats he loved to introduce into his painting. His later work—his Rhine Maidens and all his allegorical figures—are a sufficient proof of this.

Fantin, with Baudelaire and Manet, attended Delacroix's funeral in the cemetery of Père-Lachaise. To their surprise, the attendance at the grave-side was very small, and the three friends were coming dejectedly away when they saw the undertaker's men carrying, like a bundle of old clothes, the academic robes of Delacroix, which his relatives had negligently left behind.

Fantin was outraged by this insult to the memory of

such a master and conceived the idea of painting a picture
in which the leading realists and their supporters should
be found offering homage to the great romantic. Baudelaire suggested an apotheosis to include Shakespeare,
Goethe, Byron, and all the writers by whom Delacroix
had been inspired; but Fantin, after several attempts to
introduce historical, and even allegorical figures, decided
to follow the example of Frans Hals and to paint his group
in contemporary costume.

Baudelaire and Manet had naturally to be included;
Duranty brought in Champfleury, the champion of Courbet; Legros and Whistler arranged to go to Paris a fortnight before the Salon, and Whistler wrote to Fantin
asking him to reserve "two good places." Louis Cordier,
Albert de Balleroy, and Bracquemond—all artists—completed the group.

Whistler stands out from the rest, not only by his good
place, but by his extreme elegance and by the sprightliness
of his attitude. Manet, Bracquemond, Legros look like
painters and nothing else; Champfleury looks like an elder
statesman, Baudelaire like an ecclesiastic. Whistler is the
military officer in mufti, and so indeed he always remained.

As a man of 1863 he found a natural place in such a
group, but Champfleury and Baudelaire must have been a
trifle surprised to find themselves together. It was at first
intended to include Rossetti, and he was left out only because he was unable to find time to give sittings. Fantin,

no more than anyone else, was able to perceive the widely divergent paths which some of his friends were destined to follow, and it is natural for a young man to exaggerate the intellectual solidarity of those who form his immediate circle. Rossetti, of course, was merely the friend of a friend, but Fantin was willing to take him on trust from Whistler. Perhaps he did not know Rossetti's opinion of his friends' work. In a letter to his mother in November, 1864 (that is to say, while "L'Hommage à Delacroix" was being painted), Rossetti wrote: "The new French school is simple putrescence and decomposition. There is a man named Manet (to whose studio I was taken by Fantin) whose pictures are, for the most part, mere scrawls, and who seems to be one of the lights of the school. Courbet, the head of it, is not much better." Rossetti's connection with French art was precisely nothing. Even Whistler's connection was growing steadily less.

A distinguished modern critic,[2] who is no friend to Whistler, contends that, even in "The White Girl," he was nothing but "an unfrocked Pre-Raphaelite."

Unmodern . . . or, in plain words, insufficient, is the conception, the phantomlike yet insupportably material quality of the apparition, the incapacity for making a body stand on its legs in any medium, and for preserving the relation of the parts in the at-

[2] See "Modern Art," by Julius Meier-Graefe (London, 1908), Vol. II, p. 201.

tempted plasticity. The whole tendency to give a spiritual appearance without any spiritual essence, the
ghostly by means of a trap-door, is Rossettian. The
artist simply asserts what he has to demonstrate,
reproduces his mystery instead of creating it and making it effectual. It is the trick of a juggler at a fair.

A more obvious resemblance to Rossetti's work is seen
in the painting which Whistler called "La Princesse du
Pays de la Porcelaine." We have seen that it was at the
Ionides house at Tulse Hill that Whistler first found himself in the Rossetti circle, and Tulse Hill was a complete
nursery of "Stunners." For the Pre-Raphaelites the term
had an almost technical significance.[3] It signified almost
any object of esthetic rapture, but in particular women,
women who were an inspiration to poet and artist, beautiful or tragic women; the whole of Rossetti's sensual, spiritual cult summed up in a single word of schoolboy slang.
Lizzie Siddal, Rossetti's dead wife, Fanny Cornforth, his
mistress, Janie Morris, Georgina Burne-Jones and her sisters, Agnes Poynter, Alice Lockwood Kipling, and Louie
Baldwin, Emily Knewstub, Kate Howell—all were "Stunners." But at Tulse Hill there were several in the Ionides
family itself: Aglaia Chariclea and her niece Mary Casa-
vetti and (most important of all) the two Spartali girls,
Christine (afterwards Countess Edmond de Cahen) and
Marie (Mrs. Stillman).

[3] See an amusing article with excellent photographs: "Stunners," by
Violet Hunt, Artwork, No. 22 (1930).

ROSSETTI AND THE INFLUENCE OF JAPAN

Marie Spartali was Rossetti's pupil and frequently posed for him. Her sister Christine posed for Whistler's painting of "La Princesse du Pays de la Porcelaine." The two sisters were, naturally enough, of the same type of Mediterranean beauty, with full red lips and masses of black hair, and it would be strange indeed if Whistler had avoided in this picture a certain similarity to the work of Rossetti. However, so sound a critic as Léonce Bénédite thought that the resemblance was not one of type alone, but that Whistler abandoned for once his habitual manner of working, and assimilated his technique to that of the older man. But the picture is less remarkable for what evidence it shows of Whistler's debt to Rossetti than as a plain proof of the influence of the Japanese.

It used to be thought that Rossetti had introduced him to Japan. The very reverse is true, for it was from Whistler that the whole tide of Japanese influence flowed to modify interior decoration and to color the Esthetic Movement. William Rossetti, in his "Reminiscences," states quite clearly that when his brother took Tudor House the Japanese mania had not begun. "It was Mr. Whistler who first called my brother's attention to Japanese art: he possessed two or three woodcut books, some colored prints and a screen or two. . . . I have heard him say, and perhaps with accuracy, that Édouard Manet was the 'head and front' of Japonnerie, and I know that at an early date in the movement Tissot was a keen collector." Rossetti became a keen collector also, and amassed great quantities of china, but the craze had singularly little effect on his art He did not even make use of Japanese objects in his pic tures; still less was he influenced by oriental ideals of paint ing. Whistler was for many years the only "Japanese' artist in England.

The impulse, once again, came from France, and the story is sufficiently curious to be worth setting out in some detail. In the year 1856, that is to say two years after Whistler's arrival in Paris, the etcher Bracquemond was according to his custom, taking some plates to Delâtre to be printed. While he was in the shop he noticed a smal' book with a limp red paper cover. It had come as packing in a parcel of porcelain sent by some of Delâtre's French acquaintances in Japan. Bracquemond opened it, found it full of woodcuts of the kind now familiar but then almost unknown to Europe. He was fascinated by the vigor of the little figures and the beautiful arrangement of each print He was more excited by the little book than by all his visit to great picture galleries. He tried to persuade Delâtre to give it to him, then to sell it, but the printer was obdurate Bracquemond left the shop without the book.

A year or more later he was visiting the wood-engraver Lavieille, and beheld the same little book he had coveted *chez* Delâtre. Lavieille did not want to part with it either but Bracquemond resolved to tempt him. He had in his possession a copy of Papillon's book on wood-engraving—

the bible of wood-engravers—in which the dignity of their craft is proclaimed. This volume naturally appealed to Lavieille, and Bracquemond offered to trade it for the little red book. Lavieille consented, and Bracquemond kept the flimsy, fiber-bound volume in his pocket and carried it about with him for the rest of his life.

The Japanese influence is now so much of a commonplace that we find it hard to understand the force of the revelation in the late fifties of the last century. The eighteenth century had seen collections of objects brought from the Orient, and the furniture and woven stuffs of that period had been profoundly influenced, but nothing was known of the Japanese color-print, for the very good reason that it hardly then existed. The great development of the Ukiyoye school, with its *contemporary* subject matter, did not begin until the end of the century, and by 1860 it was in full decline. Hokusai and Hiroshige were early nineteenth-century artists, both great in a popular art which the Japanese themselves somewhat despised. It was one of the volumes of the Mangwa of Hokusai that Bracquemond had discovered in Delâtre's shop.

It is quite possible that the other artists, including Whistler, had seen the little book when Delâtre had it; it is more likely that Bracquemond himself was responsible for their initiation, for he showed the book to everyone, and his enthusiasm was infectious. A certain Madame de Soye opened a shop in the rue de Rivoli for the sale of

Chinese and Japanese goods, and Bracquemond and his friends were frequent visitors. The Goncourt brothers went, and Baudelaire, James Tissot, afterwards famous as an oriental collector, even Villot, keeper of the Louvre, and of course Whistler and Fantin. Later came Burty, the critic, Degas, and Zola; the latter was so far bitten by the craze for Japanese prints that he had the staircase of his house hung with some of the less reticent examples—the "furious fornications" which excited the interest of Mr. George Moore when he went to pay the novelist his first visit.

Whistler carried his enthusiasm to London and soon both Rossettis (Dante Gabriel and his brother William) were collecting oriental objects. At first William had to do his buying in the rue de Rivoli, but soon a shop was opened in London by the firm, long since defunct, of Farmer and Rogers in Regent Street. Mr. Lasenby Liberty was an assistant in the shop, and when the opportunity came he set up for himself on the opposite side of the street. His shop is there yet, a lasting monument to the revelation which came to Bracquemond and the missionary zeal of Whistler. Both Whistler and Rossetti were assisted in their collecting by the highly cultivated dealer Murray Marks.

The exact date of the opening of La Porte Chinoise, as the Paris shop was called, seems in dispute, and the point is not merely academic, for it would be interesting to know whether Whistler was already acquainted with Japanese art when he painted "The Music Room."

[ 114 ]

The use of the silhouette and the curious perspective seem to suggest oriental influences, but whether that is so or not these oriental influences soon afterwards took complete possession of him and for a time threatened to submerge his art.

He became known in Chelsea as "the Japanese artist," and it was under that name that he was pointed out to Walter Greaves, as Whistler sat painting in the window of his first house in Lindsey Row. The Greaves family also lived in Lindsey Row, in a little white house which used to jut out at the end of the larger building, and the father, a prosperous boat-builder, had known Turner. There was an artistic tradition in the family, and it was inevitable that sooner or later the Greaves boys should get to know Whistler. "Tinnie," their sister, sat to Whistler, and Walter and Harry rowed him about the river, carried his painting materials, and worked in his studio. They accompanied him to an art school in Limerston Street where a nude model posed in the evening. Whistler made studies in chalk on brown paper, and the Greaveses learned what they could from him as he worked. But it was his later painting which was to have most influence on their own.[4]

Whistler's enthusiasm for Japan continued unabated, and when Fantin proposed to paint another group picture

[4] That influence was almost wholly unfortunate. Walter Greaves was a genuine *naïf* diverted and spoiled by Whistler's sophisticated example.

of his friends Whistler insisted on appearing in it in a Japanese robe. In this we may note the sign of separation from his French friends, for in their eyes Fantin's previous picture had been notable largely because of its acceptance of modern dress. Fantin's first idea for the new work was that it should be a blend of the allegorical and the actual, a nude female figure with men in black coats and silk hats, the whole representing *L'Hommage à la Verité*. Finally the nude figure was omitted and the picture called "Le Toast," but Fantin never liked it and finally cut it up, preserving only three of the heads, including Whistler's, which is now in America. However, it was exhibited before its destruction, Manet and Whistler facing one another as if defiantly measuring the distance which already separated their art. In Fantin's next group "Un Atelier aux Batignolles" (1870), Whistler has disappeared altogether, and Manet occupies the center of the picture. He sits painting at an easel with a group of friends round him, gazing admiringly at his work. Baudelaire and Champfleury have gone, and in their place stands Zola, Manet's prophet.

Whistler's admiration for the Japanese is strongly marked in most of the pictures painted between 1864 and 1870. In the same year as he painted the "Princesse" he was also at work on another picture: "The Lange Leizen of the Six Marks." [5]

This is one of the least satisfactory of his important

[5] A corruption of the Dutch technical term: *Lange leises,* tall damsels.

pictures. It is cluttered with Japanese accessories, yet possesses very little of the Japanese spirit.

In "The Gold Screen" even the model seems Japanese, or else Whistler, conscious perhaps of the inconsistency between a head à la Rossetti and a body swathed in Japanese garments, purposely imparted an oriental cast to the features of the sitter.

"The Balcony" (1870) is a particularly interesting picture, because it shows Whistler's Japanese figures (no longer very Japanese save by their attitudes) against a background that is already recognizable as the Thames. It was almost his last attempt to pose figures against a distant background of any kind. Henceforth his painting divides into two. The gray river background of "The Balcony" becomes a separate work of art and develops into a whole series of nocturnes. The foreground figures become the basis of his portraiture, all obviously Japanese elements being gradually eliminated.

It was not indeed until Whistler had outlived his first heady enthusiasm for Japanese art that he was able to benefit by it. At first it was Japanese motifs and Japanese accessories that interested him. His figures were clothed in kimonos, handled porcelain and waved fans, while across the front of the canvas wandered a spray of foliage, cunningly placed for its purely decorative effect. There was a moment, indeed, when the decorator threatened to engulf the artist, but that moment passed. As Whistler

[ 117 ]

penetrated more and more into an understanding of oriental art, its influence upon his own work became less obvious and more profound. His composition was modified. His backgrounds grew flat, and a love of the silhouette replaced the earlier interest in modeling which he had learned from Courbet. The Japanese prints which he studied so eagerly taught him, by the limitations of their own technique, a valuable lesson. The color woodcut, by its very nature, tends to simplicity of color, for every new color means the cutting of another block. Just as the artist of the Ukiyoye arranged his inks before he started, so Whistler arranged the colors on his palet, and saw that they formed a harmony. A harmony of color applied to a decorative and rhythmical arabesque was henceforward to be his ideal in art. He had found his manner. He had arrived in 1870 at the perfect accord of his powers, at the period of his greatest portraits.

The sixties, however, had not been for Whistler a mere tranquil schooling in the secrets of Japanese art. They were the most adventurous years of his life, the years moreover in which his character, as well as his art, set in a characteristic mold which was never to be broken. We must retrace our steps a little to consider some of the events that brought this about.

# CHAPTER V

## MAKING ENEMIES

UNTIL about half-way through the sixties, Whistler appeared to be carrying all before him. Success had come to him, in spite of opposition, in both England and France. In both countries he was looked upon as one of the rising young artists. He had many friends with whom to spend his leisure, and the sympathetic Jo to keep house for him. They often lacked ready money, but that is to be expected during the early years of any artist, and Jo was the last person to be discouraged by so familiar a state of affairs. Known to the public as Mrs. Abbott, she traded his sketches for him in Bond Street, wrote his letters and, in general, acted as his agent.

In return, although it may have seemed at the time just another task for her, he depicted her beautiful body and glorious hair in some of the most successful of his paintings and etchings. Even in monochrome the glow of the hair is not extinguished; for in his etching of her head and shoulders the shadowed face is surrounded by long thick strands full of light and color. Whistler was very exacting, and Jo must often have been almost worn out with posing, but, when after a long day, sometime in 1863, she collapsed exhausted into a deep chair, the tireless needle of the artist still went on, tracing upon the copper the outlines of her voluminous skirt, her tight bodice with the full sleeves, and her tired face resting against the living cushion formed by the masses of her hair. This was the drypoint which Whistler called "Weary," and it must have seemed to Jo—for she understood these things—a true recompense for all she had done for him, and all she was still to suffer at his hands. On the whole they seem to have been very happy, and Whistler looked back on this period of his life with a tenderness which he did not always display toward the past.

When domestic amusement palled there was always Cremorne, a few hundred yards west from where Whistler's own house stood. There is still in that part of Chelsea a public-house known as the World's End, and there has been a tavern there at least since the time of Congreve, who introduced it as a place of rendezvous into "Love for Love." The narrow World's End Passage still straggles from the river to the tavern, but beyond it, where wharves and shabby streets now stand, once lay Chelsea Farm, a residence of Selina, Countess of Huntingdon, Whitefield's "noble and elect lady." But more pagan times were at hand, and there is an irony of fortune in the fact that it was Lady Huntingdon's successor, the exemplary Philadelphia Hannah, Lady Cremorne, the great-granddaughter

L'HOMMAGE À DELACROIX: *By Fantin-Latour. In the Musée du Louvre.*

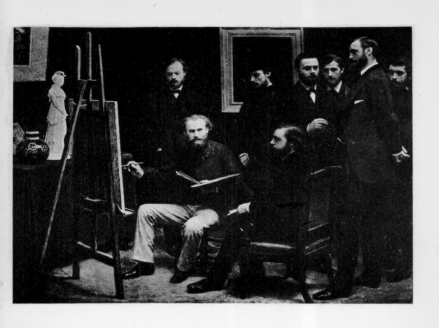

UN ATELIER AUX BATIGNOLLES:
*By Fantin=Latour. In the Musée du
Luxembourg.*

of William Penn and the friend of Queen Charlotte, who was destined to give her name to the famous and disreputable gardens.

An athletic club occupied the farm in the eighteen-thirties, but in 1845 the gardens were opened to the public and soon gained a deserved reputation for rowdiness. Vauxhall was sold by auction in 1859 just when Whistler was thinking of settling in London, and the pictures which had hung in the supper boxes were transferred to the banqueting hall at Cremorne. They were the only trace of the elegance of Vauxhall which ever appeared at the unfashionable resort farther west. Cremorne never attracted London society, and was always looked upon by the respectable as "low."

Whistler, however, was happily able to take his pleasures where he found them, and after the Bal Bullier, Cremorne was not too low, but too respectable. Still there was a crowd, which he loved, and there were fireworks, showers of sparks, brilliantly golden against the velvet blue of night above the river. He stored his memory with these sights for the time when he should come to paint the nocturnes.

On these jaunts Jo was not his only companion, for his haphazard house was full of women, models and whatnot; and their quarrels were not confined to the home, but sometimes provided such disturbances at Cremorne that the whole party was turned out. Whistler was still a

[ 121 ]

bohemian, not the sophisticated, self-conscious bohemian he was afterwards to become, but the kind whose front door was never shut, unless the duns were too insistent, and whose table was never empty, however unpaid trades-men might blaspheme. That he enjoyed such a life is a proof, at least at that time, of his bohemianism, for it would have driven the mere pretender mad.

Whistler, however, had a friend beside whose bo-hemianism his own sinks out of sight: the astounding and irrepressible Howell. Charles Augustus Howell was an adventurer with a flamboyant plausibility that amounted to genius, and he got himself so completely entangled with the history of art in England in the second half of the nineteenth century that it is almost impossible to read the biography of any artist of the period without coming across his name.

His origins were obscure; perhaps they were Portu-guese. He himself always claimed to be related to the best families in Portugal and in evening dress he wore across his shirt front the red ribbon of the Order of Christ. He boasted that he was mixed up in the Orsini conspiracy against Napoleon III, and he moved perpetually in an at-mosphere of mystery and intrigue which his artist friends found immensely exciting.

He was a powerfully built man with a strong face, high cheekbones, and the jaw of a prize-fighter; but his dark eyes were alive with intelligence, and his conversational gifts were extraordinary. His complexion was swarthy, almost oriental; he wore a slight mustache (in the days before mustaches were fashionable) and he held a lighted cigarette perpetually in his closed teeth.

His first victim was Ruskin, who, in spite of his mother's strong distrust of the man, made Howell his private secretary. From 1865 until 1868, Howell had the dispensing of Ruskin's bounty in his own hands. Rossetti was one of Ruskin's protégés, and when Ruskin trusted Howell no longer, the latter turned to Rossetti and became, for a time, indispensable to him.

Rossetti had a shrewder eye than Ruskin and he soon realized that Howell was not entirely honest; but his moral standards were laxer and his tolerance wider than Ruskin's, and Howell amused him.

There's a Portuguese person named Howell,
Who lays on his lies with a trowel;
    When I goggle my eyes
    And start with surprise,
It's at monstrous big lies told by Howell.

It was at Rossetti's that Whistler met him, and he too was amused and attracted. A flash of his own seventeenth-century sympathies, his revolt against the drabness of the modern world, come out in his description of Howell as "the Gil Blas Robinson Crusoe hero out of his proper time, a creature of top boots and plumes, splendidly flamboyant."

At the height of the Blue China craze Howell did both
Rossetti's and Whistler's shopping, as well as a little collecting for himself. He also acted as agent for Swinburne
until Theodore Watts rescued the poet from his clutches.
But acquaintance with Howell was not pure loss, for he
was a marvelous salesman and disposed of pictures for both
Whistler and Rossetti. He was always bursting with some
new scheme. He broke in horses, he salved ships, he furnished people's houses, always making some illicit profit.
With half the ingenuity and energy that he devoted to
shady practices he could have made an honest fortune.

He had a handsome swaggering way which many
women found irresistible, and his house in Putney was full
of them. His wife "Kittie" seems to have been a generous
cheerful soul, willing to overlook all her husband's irregularity. Whistler was often at the house, joking with the
women, arranging some deal with Howell or playing drafts
with an old Neapolitan who had settled on the establishment—no one knew why. The high-spirited atmosphere
of the place appealed to him. He was, at this period of his
life, somewhat promiscuous himself. That Jo was not his
only mistress is certain, for the boy whom she brought up
and who was with her at Whistler's funeral was always
referred to by the artist as "an infidelity to Jo."

Yet, in spite of all distractions, she was for many years
the center of his domestic existence. She had a child sometime in the early sixties, and her sister was brought in to

act as nurse-maid; but the dates of these early happenings are very uncertain, and it is not known what became of it.

In 1865 she was again Whistler's model for one of the finest of his paintings—the picture known as the "Little White Girl." The pose is Japanese, and so is the spray of blossom that strays into the picture from the bottom right-hand corner, and the fan in the girl's hand and the porcelain on the mantelpiece, but the artist has put into the picture a tenderness rarely found in his work. The "lost spirit" of the first "White Girl" has become human and found a home, and that home is Whistler's own house in Lindsey Row. Here is no room hung with white, but the familiar background of both their lives, the fireplace just as it was, the overmantel as they used to have it, and, re-flected in the mirror, the somewhat melancholy face he had come to know so well.

Swinburne saw the picture, and was moved to write a poem about it, a poem which Whistler liked so much that he had it pasted on the sides of the frame:

> Come snow, come wind or thunder
>    High up in air,
> I watch my face, and wonder
>    At my bright hair;
> Nought else exalts or grieves
> The rose at heart, that heaves
>    With love of its own leaves and lips that pair.

[ 125 ]

She knows not loves that kissed her
    She knows not where.
Art thou the ghost, my sister,
    White sister there,
Am I the ghost, who knows?
My hand, a fallen rose,
    Lies snow-white on white snows, and takes no
    care.

I cannot see what pleasures
    Or what pains were;
What pale new loves and treasures
    New years will bear;
What beam will fall, what shower,
What grief or joy for dower;
    But one thing knows the flower; the flower is
    fair.

The painting was exhibited in the Royal Academy of
1865. To Whistler's surprise and annoyance, the English
critics who had praised his previous work found many
faults in the "Little White Girl." It seemed strange to
them, even "bizarre," although it was surely less so than
the first "White Girl." Only W. M. Rossetti found in it
anything to praise.

Just as he had turned to England when France rejected
him, so now, in his disappointment, he turned to France.
But the French soon forget an artist who is not working
in their midst, and for them the first requisite of a work
of art, then as now, is to have been produced in Paris. To

the conservative he was just another bad painter, to the
progressive he had simply fallen out of the "Movement."
It was not until twenty years later that French criticism
awoke once more to the existence of Whistler, and then
he was no longer a revolutionary but something approaching an old master; that is, a painter whose achievements
are accepted in their own convention and whose esthetic
opinions have ceased to have any importance.

Aware of the gulf which separated him from the Pre-
Raphaelites, and made conscious of the widening gap
between his own art and that of his French contemporaries,
Whistler felt himself increasingly alone. His proud and
sensitive nature drew in upon itself, with results which are
quickly seen both in his work and in his temperament.
It is sometime in the middle sixties that a curious change
seems to take place in his character—a change for the
worse. He had always been "difficult," but strangers who
had not yet offended him were more conscious of his
charm. He seemed at one time to have a genius for friendship, and was always dreaming of groups and societies,
the members pledged to fight one another's battles. At
first it was the "Plawd," then a smaller group to consist
of Fantin, Legros, and himself. Perhaps it was when he
realized that such associations are always unstable that a
certain bitterness entered into his relationship with old
friends, that he resolved to stand alone and attract public
attention by any means he could. The eccentricity which

had once been mere high spirits hardened into a pose, for he had discovered that the idiosyncrasies which passed without comment in Paris were the source of considerable publicity in London. The more ordinary people were outraged by his departures from conventional attire and behavior the more they talked. Whistler began to like it; there even came a time when he could not live without it.

But there was perhaps a more profound reason for the change in his character: his attitude to the Civil War in America. If anyone might have been expected to hurry back to his ancestral Virginia to offer his services to the Confederacy, it was surely Whistler. There is only one reason which might have justified him for taking no part in the conflict. He was an artist. Fantin, when asked what he did in the war of 1870-71, replied that he hid in the cellar. "I'm a coward, I am!" There is even a certain dignity in such a reply which places it beside Euclid's "Do not disturb my figures." But Whistler spent his life claiming to be something besides an artist. He claimed to be a gentleman. "An officer and a gentleman" would be nearer his own conception of himself, and his sense of honor was the punctilious exacting kind which survived into our own day among the duelists of the Prussian military caste. Whistler wanted to have it both ways, to claim at one and the same time the privilege of the artist and the privilege of the gentleman. His excessive touchiness had something morbid about it, a morbidity which can perhaps be traced to his

action, or lack of it, in the Civil War. On such a supposi-
tion can be explained easily enough what is otherwise inexplicable: the fantastic expedition to Valparaiso.

After the close of the war, London was full of those
who had fought for the South and been ruined in the
process. Disgruntled officers of Lee's and Jackson's army
were everywhere, and Whistler naturally saw much of
them. His brother, Dr. William Whistler, had been
through the war as a surgeon on the Confederate side. He
had even had the excitement of bringing dispatches to
England, which, owing to the blockade, he was compelled
to do through the hostile northern states, finally sailing
from New York to Liverpool. It is possible that Whistler
might have returned with him, but his mother was in
London also, having run the blockade, and before Dr.
Whistler himself could bring his furlough to an end the
war was over.

Whistler always admired men of action. With his
mother and brother he visited the Continent and met
Courbet again, and Courbet too was a man of action, and
had been on the barricades. In November, 1865, Whistler
was back in London and saw more Southerners every day.
No wonder his mind was exalted with the fumes of heroism. He did not know himself how it happened, but suddenly it was decided to form an expedition to help the
Chileans, and the Peruvians too, against the Spaniards.
Whistler sailed from Southampton for Panama early in

1866, and was in Valparaiso in time for the Spanish bombardment.

Of course the expedition accomplished nothing. The whole episode was farcical, and Whistler afterwards described in amusing terms how he and his companions scampered out of the town on horseback—"The riding was splendid, and I, as a West Point man, was head of the procession"—in order to escape the leisurely shelling of the Spanish gunboats. In later years, Whistler liked to imagine that this was not the whole story, that he had, in fact, done something heroic, had climbed onto one of the defending gunboats and received his "baptism of fire amid a rain of shot and shell." He related as much to his disciple Theodore Roussel, but said not a word about it to the Pennells, who were his chosen biographers, and the story is chiefly interesting as an example of how long the memory of Valparaiso rankled in Whistler's mind.

He did not altogether waste his time there. A Mr. McQueen put him up for his club, and from the club window as night was falling, Whistler painted a view of Valparaiso harbor with the lights of the vessels gleaming through the dusk. It was the first of the nocturnes, one of five painted during the expedition; but Whistler had not gone out to South America to paint, but to fight the Spaniards, and he must have felt rather a fool.

On the journey back he was excessively irritable, and becoming annoyed with the airs of a Haitian Negro who

was on board, he vented upon him all the martial ardor
which had not been expended against the Spanish fleet.
This was the Marquis de Marmalade episode of which
Whistler was fond of talking, although some of his friends,
like William Rossetti, were frank enough to tell him what
they thought of it. The captain appears to have been of
Rossetti's opinion, and Whistler was confined to his cabin
for the rest of the voyage. However, on arrival in London,
his high spirits broke out again, and he had a fight with
some unknown man on the platform at Waterloo.

Whistler had made an unfortunate discovery: that he
could use his fists to some purpose. Although small, he had
powerful shoulders and long arms. In the studio in Paris
he had despised his friends' boxing bouts; now he took
lessons from a professional in London. In an age grown
unaccustomed to such feats, he found that the unexpected-
ness of his assault often made it damaging to his victim
and harmless to himself. He found he could be quarrel-
some with comparative impunity, and the knowledge did
him very little good.

In 1867 he was in Paris for the Exhibition, and was
walking one day through a narrow street in the Quartier
Latin when a workman dropped some plaster on his
clothes. In Pennell's beautiful phrase, Whistler "met the
offense in the only way possible according to his code."
That code the workman was, perhaps, incapable of understanding, and he invoked the aid of the magistrate. Still,

it is to be hoped, in accordance with his code, Whistler claimed the protection of the American minister, and was released.

However, a few days later he met Seymour Haden in the same district and, having accumulated a number of grievances against him by this time, pushed him through a plate-glass window. Whistler, by the justice of the gods, was brought before the same magistrate as before, and this time outside influence did not avail to save him from a fine.

From now onwards, the breach between Haden and Whistler was impassable. Haden was outraged at the insolence of his brother-in-law, and when he got back to London he rushed to the Burlington Fine Arts Club, of which they were both members, and threatened to resign unless Whistler were expelled. Whistler *was* expelled, and the two Rossettis, considering that he had been hardly used, left with him.

Still unsatisfied, Whistler picked a quarrel with Legros. It is thought that the subject of dispute was a woman. In answer to Whistler's accusation—whatever it was—Legros gave him the lie. He received a violent blow on the face and never spoke to Whistler again for the rest of his life. Neither did Haden.

Early in 1867 Whistler moved into No. 2 Lindsey Row, now 96 Cheyne Walk, and gave a house-warming to which the Rossettis were invited. It must have seemed a strange contrast to Tudor House, for he had decorated it in accordance with his own ideas, and Whistler, whatever else he lacked, had superb taste as a decorator. He would have none of the overcrowding so typical of the period, none of the pseudo-antique chairs, the faked medieval windows, the litter of art objects, the palms in pots. His taste for simplicity antedated that of the rest of England by more than a generation. His dining-room was painted blue with darker blue woodwork and doors. A few purple Japanese fans were cunningly placed on walls and ceiling. The Japanese fan afterwards became so vulgarized and overused that it is hard for us to realize it once had the charm of novelty. But in 1867 the Japanese craze, so far as the general public was concerned, was only just beginning, for it was only in that year that the Paris Exhibition drew attention to Japanese art. Whistler's drawing-room was flesh-color with white and yellow doors and strips of Japanese embroidery on the walls, but Whistler grew easily bored with the actual work of decoration, and it was not until the immediate prospect of a party drove him to action that he got the Greaveses in to help him finish it. Even so, it did not dry in time. The studio was gray with black woodwork, with no attempt at imitating the show studios of fashionable painters, with their semi-oriental or pseudo-classical architecture, their wealth of knickknacks.

In his art he was being subjected to a new and unexpected influence. His quarrel with Legros had broken up the "Society of Three" which Whistler had dreamed of forming. Fantin, safe on the other side of the Channel, was still his friend, and Whistler looked about, consciously or unconsciously, for someone to take Legros's place. The new friend was the painter Albert Moore.

Whistler wrote exultantly to Fantin:

"In reality, we two march in the van. It is as at the big races, as at the Derby. The thoroughbred wins! I think that we may now be sure of it. The field is ours. The pure breed reappears in us."

Fantin, living in Paris, must have raised his eyebrows a little at so complete a forgetfulness of his own friends. Was not Manet in the race too? But the rest of the letter was even more surprising.

"'There is only one other," continued Whistler, "worthy of us. This third is young Moore, of whom I have often spoken to you."

Albert Moore, one of a whole family of painters, was born in 1841. He was extremely precocious and his first paintings were exhibited in 1859 when he was only eighteen, but it was not until 1865 that his individual style emerged, when he abandoned his earlier biblical illustrations for a series of "arrangements" as free from subject as Whistler's own: groups of young women, of a pseudo-classical type, clad in clinging or diaphanous garments, and grouped harmoniously on antique marble seats or posing pleasantly amid sprays of flowers.

Perhaps it was the lack of subject, the purely decorative aspect of his painting, which attracted Whistler. Perhaps it was Moore's character, as independent as his own and equally in revolt against the Academies. But, whatever the cause, he liked Moore and, for a time, was much in his company. They visited the British Museum together and admired the Tanagra statuettes.

Moore had discovered the resemblance that exists between certain English feminine types and late classical sculpture, and upon this discovery had based the construction of a whole "five-o'clock-tea antiquity." The phrase has been used of Alma-Tadema, but it is even more applicable to Moore. Indeed, Alma-Tadema and Leighton were both influenced by Moore, and so for a time was Whistler himself.

The first painting in which this is manifest is the "Symphonie en blanc No. 3," which is a blend of the Japanese influences that he had not quite shaken off and the neo-classical ideals introduced by Moore. He wrote enthusiastically to Fantin to relate the progress of the new work. Jo was to be the "White Girl" once more, but another figure was to be introduced as a contrast—not too much of a contrast lest the harmony of the symphony should be destroyed: "A blond head, a robe of yellow-white silk, the kind known as foulard. A few purple flowers, fallen to the ground near the yellow robe . . . a very delicate gray background." He took immense pains with the silhouette and the arrangement of the two girls' out-stretched arms on the sofa. His draftsmanship was always less *correct* than Moore's, but his sense of design was in-finitely more subtle, and his feeling for color more delicate. Still under the influence of Moore, he made sketches for six "schemes," compositions, for the most part, of nude figures, singularly slender and seductive, touched with an eighteenth-century grace, an oriental languor and a Helle-nistic elegance; but it was in his pastels and his lithographs that the effect of the younger man's friendship was long-est visible.

Whistler produced a whole series of small studies of nude or slightly draped figures done on brown paper with pastel colors or very liquid paint. The models he chose were always young and slender to the point of fragility, and the artist clothed them—when he clothed them at all—in flimsy draperies through which the pale flesh gleams. They stand, or crouch, or half recline with a seductive elegance, which is partly due to their own adolescent grace and partly to the caressing hand of the artist sketching in the outlines of their immature forms. They remind one somewhat of the little pen drawings scattered through the text of La Vie Parisienne, not La Vie Parisienne of Whistler's day but of our own, which is only to say that Whistler's taste in women has filtered down and that his vision has become a commonplace. Whistler's figures are still seductive; Moore's are not.

[ 136 ]

THE WAVE: *By Gustave Courbet.*
*In the Musée du Louvre.*

THE BLUE WAVE: *In the possession*
*of A. A. Pope, Esq.*

It was in company with Moore that Whistler began to go about at night for the express purpose of noting effects of twilight and darkness, and to develop his visual memory in the way recommended to his pupils by Lecoq de Boisbaudran. Sometimes the two would get the Greaveses to row them about all night, or start very early in the morning in order to breakfast with Howell at Putney.

The notes were made on brown paper in black and white chalk, and all the tints and values were memorized in order to be worked later into an "Arrangement" or a "Nocturne." It is interesting to note that the first mention of these two famous terms occurs in 1872, Whistler afterwards bringing his earlier pictures into the scheme. Not only was each picture to be an arrangement, but the whole of his work was to be seen in retrospect as the embodiment of one idea.

He was conscious of that fascination exercised by musical terms over many who are essentially unmusical. Whistler had no comprehension of music at all—the evidence of those who knew him best is conclusive on this point—but that mattered little. The artist has to raise his imaginative temperature somehow; he needs some kind of stimulant before he can create, and Whistler probably selected one of those least harmful to the pictorial artist. Rossetti was less fortunate in his drugs. He chose to induce the creative mood by soaking himself in Italian poetry, with the result that too often (but not always) his art is

[ 137 ]

more literature than painting. "Why trouble to paint the picture at all?" said Whistler, when Rossetti showed him a preliminary sonnet which was to form its subject. "Why not simply frame the sonnet?" In this he showed a sound instinct, and his musical conception of painting, if it limited his scope, certainly preserved him from considerable danger.

There can, of course, be no exact analogy between an art which exists in space and an art which unrolls in time, and Whistler did not strain the comparison unduly. Still less did he allow himself to be deprived of other colors by the one he had chosen for his principal, and he rightly rebuked the foolish critic who misinterpreted his intentions, in one of the most successful of his sarcastic paragraphs:

"Not precisely a symphony in white . . . for there is a dress . . . brown hair, etc. . . . another with reddish hair . . . and of course there is the flesh-color of the complexions."

*Bon Dieu!* did this wise person expect white hair and chalked faces? And does he then, in his astounding consequence, believe that a symphony in F. contains no other note, but shall be a continual repetition of F. F. F.? . . . Fool!

The musical notation served two purposes. It served to remind the artist himself of the need for simplicity and of the peril of subordinating general effect to local color; and it served to remind the public that, whatever else he was trying to do, he was not attempting to tell a story. Hence his "Arrangements," "Harmonies," and the rest, which visitors to public exhibitions at first found so puzzling.

Whistler had arrived at that most critical period of an artist's life when he begins to find his own individual style free for the first time from the influences which have served to mold it. He had broken away from Courbet, he had ceased to be influenced in the slightest degree by Rossetti, and he had assimilated the Japanese so completely that, although their methods of arranging the subject were constantly in his mind, their knickknacks disappeared forever from his paintings. He even abandoned after a time that decorative use of a spray of leaves over one corner of a picture which is so common in oriental art. The influence of Moore grew gradually less and less until it persisted only in his minor works.

The essence of his method was simplification. It is probable, as he was a shortsighted man, that he *saw* things simplified, that when the model stood a few feet away from him he lost sight of everything but the contour and the main tones. It has been suggested that he was so sensitive to color that he thought he was painting scarlet when he was really painting pale pink, and that his browns and grays had for him an intensity which the normal eye failed to see. The explanation is a trifle fantastic, although it might serve to explain his love of twilight. Perhaps it is

[ 139 ]

not unkind to suggest that he painted in low tones because low tones were very much easier to harmonize. The shrill concert of the early Italians, the full trumpet notes of Rubens seem to have been beyond the capacity of nineteenth-century artists. The Pre-Raphaelites left the harmony to look after itself; Whistler cut out everything in the orchestra but the wood-wind.

There were other considerations. Pennell used to grow particularly angry when anyone suggested that Whistler could not draw. He even goes so far as to say that Whistler drew better than Ingres. Whistler himself had no such delusions, and was honest enough to lament his incapacity in his letters to Fantin. The test of an artist's draftsmanship is his power of drawing hands and feet in a convincing manner. Nearly all the attempts in Whistler's pictures are weak in outline and uncertain in modeling. His figures often float over the ground rather than rest solidly upon it. And he simplified his contours by applying to the shape of the human figure his own canons of elegance.

Painters like Rembrandt who love modeling, especially the modeling of the human face, like to illuminate their figures from the side. The effect is most dramatic, but Whistler wisely eschewed it. He lit his figures directly from the front and so reduced their interior modeling to a minimum. His figures resemble those of actors in the old-fashioned theater, purposely *flattened* in order not to conflict with the flat-painted scenery.

As early as the painting of "The Music Room" we find Whistler aiming at the effect of a flat silhouette. To make the most of it he progressively simplified his background, until nothing remained but a single line representing the dado on the back wall. The "Mother" and the "Carlyle," considered as compositions, are nothing but cunningly placed silhouettes, and if he could do no more than this his art was not much more than that of the skilful photographer.

For Whistler, however, there remained the further problem of color. As we have seen he noticeably reduced the possible margin of error by restricting his palet to a narrow range. His exquisite taste did the rest. The main labor of harmonizing was over when he stood at the canvas ready to begin; the colors were already arranged on the elaborate table palet which he used all his life. He is known, for one of his seascapes, to have spent three days in mixing his colors and something over an hour in painting the picture. There is nothing reprehensible in such a system, but it had its difficulties when applied to the painting of portraits.

To obtain the unity of surface which he needed, Whistler used very liquid paint. The first sitting was spent in posing the model and in deciding on the elements of the projected "harmony." The figure was then lightly brushed in. When the second sitting was over the picture appeared to be finished, and many would have been glad to take it as it was rather than face the risk of its being spoiled, as frequently happened, by further work. Whistler, however, was unsatisfied, and for this we must respect his artistic integrity. As Cocteau says, when the sketch appears to be complete and all the painter's friends implore him to do no more, "then the real artist tries his luck." Whistler was quite willing to take the hazard—and only the most fanatical Whistlerian will deny that a large element of chance entered into the matter—till the fiftieth and the hundredth sitting. Sometimes he grew tired and renounced his project. Sometimes the sitter's strength collapsed first. Whistler took so long over one of his child-paintings that whole families sat for it from the eldest to the youngest, and then members of other families, until the original sitter returned from America, the mother of five children (a true story, this!) to find the painting still unfinished. Whistler began hundreds of portraits. He finished about a dozen; but what portraits they are!

In 1871 Whistler was at work on the most famous of all his paintings, the portrait of his mother, which is now in the Luxembourg. In this picture the system that he had been working out for himself found its full expression. The idea, the arrangement, seems to have come to him quite suddenly, for he used the back of a canvas on which he had been painting a girl's head. The pose of the sitter is too well known to need description. It is enough to say that with this simple silhouette and the narrow range of colors which Whistler allowed himself he accomplished something that he was never to surpass. The disposition of the forms is masterly, the balance perfect, and there is a tenderness and a delicacy in the handling which show the sensibility of Whistler in its most engaging aspect. Few pictures succeed in evoking so complete a sensation of resigned tranquillity.

When the picture was submitted to the hanging committee of the Royal Academy, it was decided to reject it, on what grounds it is very difficult to see. However, one of the members, Sir William Boxall, threatened to resign and stir up a scandal unless the picture were accepted. It was hung, but it was the last Whistler ever sent to the Annual Exhibition.

A few of Whistler's friends were quick to recognize the success of his mother's portrait, and one of them—a Madame Venturi—brought Carlyle to the studio, hoping that he would be induced to sit.

The meeting of Chelsea's two most famous residents, the old philosopher and the young painter, must have provided a piquant contrast—Carlyle grumpy and dour, with garments that were more like draperies than clothes, the grizzled beard, the crucified expression; and by his side the dapper little man, tight-waisted and elegantly shod, hair studiously disordered, eyeglass twinkling, gesticulating, prattling, motioning his visitor to a chair.

To Whistler, Carlyle was just an old man whom others called distinguished. He was quite willing to paint him. To Carlyle, Whistler was a lunatic with an inexplicable gift for painting. He regarded him with good-humored contempt and always referred to him as "the creature." He had broken off a long-standing friendship with Browning because the poet rode down to Chelsea in a purple coat to see him. However, there was no question of intimacy with Whistler, and even his dandyism escaped reproof. Carlyle liked the "Mother" portrait, and one morning arrived at Whistler's studio unexpectedly, sat down in a chair and told the artist to "fire away." "When you are fighting a battle or painting a picture, the only thing is to fire away!"

Whistler's theory of portraiture was not so simple, and the philosopher grew very impatient before the work was done. He wanted to know why Whistler used such small brushes, and the latter had to pretend to work with larger ones in order to convince his sitter that he was not niggling. He brushed the face in quickly; it was the coat which gave him all the trouble. Carlyle could not understand the difficulty and at last he refused to sit any more, so that the coat was painted from a model. Yet Whistler was right to take so much trouble over the coat, for its silhouette is the crux of his design.

The protrait is a pendant to the "Mother" and the scheme is almost the same, perhaps too similar not to suffer by comparison. The arrangement is as skilful as before, the pictures on the wall as cunningly placed. Of psychological insight (to use a dangerous term) there is almost nothing. Carlyle to Whistler was a tired old man, and it is as a tired old man that he has painted him.

Other pictures were in progress at the same time, for in the early seventies Whistler was at the height of his powers. He was painting Mrs. Leyland, but the story of his relations with the Leylands must be left to a later chapter. He was also painting the portrait of a daughter of W. C. Alexander—the "Miss Alexander," which many consider his finest achievement.

It is as if he had wearied of painting old age and turned with relief to the freshness of early girlhood. Here his delicacy of insight did not fail him. He had, indeed, given proof of it before, and it is no accident that the most successful of his etchings, "Annie Haden," and one of the finest of his paintings, "Miss Alexander," should deal with such similar subjects. He had portrayed Annie just as she chanced to appear before him, dressed to go out in the round hat and cape of the early sixties; but his last two portraits had taught him how important arrangement was for the success of his method, and he took infinite pains with Miss Alexander before ever touching the canvas.

Whistler was to paint the whole family including the elder daughter, the real Miss Alexander, who was dark; but the artist, after his two somber pictures, longed for a "light arrangement," and so the younger daughter Cicely, who was fair, was handed over to him to endure the misery of seventy sittings. In her portrait Whistler's love of elegance manifests itself clearly for the first time. He chose the muslin for her dress, and had much to say in the making of it. He decided where the bows should be placed and how long the frills should be. The dress was even laundered under his direction, and he got Tinnie Greaves to make a carpet of black and white tape for the little girl to stand on. He was determined that the portrait should be as *chic* as he and the *couturière* could make it.

Cicely was not at all pleased at being selected in preference to her sister. She was not yet old enough to find immortality a sufficient reward for martyrdom, and tears of weariness used to roll down her cheeks as the artist, quite oblivious of her sufferings, darted backwards and forwards to the canvas, painting his "Harmony in Gray and Green." Just as she thought he had finished he would scrape it all out and begin again.

At last it was done, and the small sitter was free to run off and play, to grow up and to grow old, leaving that exquisite image of her childhood fixed forever on the master's canvas. Never was his butterfly more appropriate. The whole painting is a miracle of lightness, and the little girl herself is like some delicate white moth poised for an instant with faintly fluttering wings. There were many things that Whistler could not do. He lacked the breadth, the scope, the largeness of vision of those earlier artists who could cover a huge wall with interlaced and firmly related figures. He lacked gusto, the joy of modeling, the excite-

ment of contrasted light and shade. He lacked the inno-
cent vision of the early Italians and the profundity of
Rembrandt. Yet he had something in exchange.

Sometime in the late sixties or early seventies, Jo disappears from Whistler's life and is replaced by the more
elegant figure of Maud Franklin. There is no record of a
quarrel, but Jo had always retained her status of model;
she seems to have had no part in Whistler's social activities.
Maud was on a different footing, and rapidly assumed the
style and title of Mrs. Whistler, although he himself always referred to her as "madame." The difference between
the two women might even be taken as typical of the
change in Whistler's art, of his growing sophistication.
There is a certain full-bloodedness in his early canvases
which disappears forever when he emerges from the influence of Courbet. Jo, with her generous proportions and her
mass of hair, was what is called "a fine woman"; Maud
was more the fine lady. Her hair, too, was ruddy, but not so
plentiful, her face was thinner; she was not so handsome,
but there was an elegance about her, a kind of slim grace
which Whistler, in his art, came to prize more and more.

Refinement and sophistication are dangerous things
for a painter, and they were dangerous to Whistler, but
in a picture like the "Miss Alexander" even his wilful self-
limitation is justified, even his desire for elegance before
all things finds its perfect expression and its complete
excuse.

[ 147 ]

## CHAPTER VI

WHISTLER never did anything better than the portraits he painted during the early seventies. This was probably the happiest part of his career, for he was at the plenitude of his powers and the hostile tide which surrounded him had not yet invaded his own peace of mind. Sitters were not yet afraid of coming to him because of the ridicule of their friends.

Nevertheless, his tastes were expensive, and he was frequently short of money. While never a spendthrift on the grand scale—for it requires a certain vulgarity to be that, and mere ostentation was never Whistler's form of vanity—he was by temperament incapable of denying himself any small luxury which came his way. Although very abstemious, he liked his wine and food to be good, and served, if possible, in old glass and on rare china. He was the right kind of collector, a man who buys beautiful things for use and buys them because he thinks them beautiful, not because they fill a niche in the history of art or because they are highly priced. But even the right kind of collecting needs money, and Whistler was never able to refuse an exquisite piece of china or some particularly elegant example of old English silver.

[ 148 ]

His hospitality, though never large, was constant, and then, as now, the pleasure of offering a really well-chosen meal, even to half a dozen guests, is one which only the rich can afford very often. Sometimes he played tricks upon his friends. He knew from experience that cheap white wine is somewhat less poisonous than cheap red wine. When his funds were low he would purchase the cheapest drinkable Graves, affix an impressive seal of colored wax to the cork, and make believe to bring up the bottle from the cellar with reverent hands.

Many descriptions have been given of his behavior at table. The meal at which he preferred to dispense hospitality was Sunday luncheon, or, as he preferred to call it, with a touch of Parisian snobbery, Sunday breakfast. Guests were invited for twelve o'clock, but when they arrived found Whistler still in bed or singing in his bath. His habitual unpunctuality was one of the things his friends had to learn to put up with. At two o'clock he would appear before his assembled guests, and the performance would begin.

Nothing is more typical of Whistler than the art with which he made even his hospitality into an occasion for the display of his personality. When the guests were seated, he would prepare some delicacy for them with his own hands. Menpes, his disciple, declares that he was an excellent cook but too fussy, and would sometimes allow a dish to grow cold while he prepared some unnecessarily elaborate sauce.

[ 149 ]

He talked the whole time, like a conjurer whose patter never ceases even when the rabbits are emerging from the hat. He ate hardly anything and was never in his chair. To see him pour wine was to witness a perfect work of art. As he got up to go round the table with the bottle—for he never allowed the wine to circulate in decanters—he would begin an anecdote, pouring into the glasses at the exact moment when a pause was most effective. He used his eye-glass in the same way to emphasize the point of his stories. He was the most artificial of conversationalists and one of the most exhilarating. Even hostile evidence bears witness to the enchantment of his talk. He gave his guests immense pleasure and himself even more. But after the feast he had to face his unfortunate tradesmen, who were unconvinced that the artist had a right to give luncheon parties at their expense.

In his difficulties he turned once more to Howell. On one occasion he was leaning out of the window of his house in Lindsey Row when he saw Howell passing, surrounded as always by women, while he strutted in the middle like the lord of the farmyard. Whistler complained of his lack of funds, and Howell had one of his inevitable inspirations—nothing felonious this time. He reminded Whistler of the plates of his old etchings—a gold mine locked up in copper. Why not take fresh impressions and sell them to the dealers? Whistler demurred, saying that his press was rusty, that he had no ink, that the plates were probably in too bad a condition. But Howell, like the jinnee in the fable, once invoked could not be so easily put off.

He strode into the house, found the plates, put the press into working order, ground fresh ink, pulled proofs, and rescued Whistler for the moment from his financial difficulties. Such a man deserved the commission that he never failed to extract for his friendly services.

He had, if unwittingly, one important effect in the development of Whistler's art. One of his friends was the woman painter, Rosa Corder. She accompanied him everywhere and was frequently with him in Whistler's home. On one such occasion the eyes of the artist fell upon her slim, elegant figure as it stood, silhouetted for a moment, against one of his black doors. For once a harmony offered itself without arrangement. Whistler begged her to pose for him in the same dress and in the same attitude, and the painting which resulted is one of the most famous of all his pictures. To look at this picture is to recapture the thrill of a discovery, to share in Whistler's excitement as Miss Corder gazed about her, head in air, in front of the black door. The hair is piled high on the head, emphasizing the purity of the profile. A line of white runs from the neck down the front of the corsage, reenforcing the vertical line. The arm hangs straight down by her side, and in her hand she carries a hat with a plume from which droops a long curved feather. One wonders why women did not flock to

[ 151 ]

the painter of such a picture as they might have hurried to the creator of some new gown—to be made more elegant.

Patrons indeed were finding their way to his studio, and other women were to be immortalized in like fashion. Chief among these was Mrs. Leyland.

It was Rossetti who first introduced Whistler to Leyland, who was attracted by him and purchased "La Princesse du Pays de la Porcelaine." This was sometime in 1867, and for ten years the profitable friendship persisted. Leyland was a remarkable man, born of poor parents in Liverpool, and he had made a career first in the employ of Bibby, the ship-owner, and then as a ship-owner himself. Throughout the nineteenth century there was a tradition of culture among the merchant princes of Liverpool, and Leyland, although a "self-made man," had talent himself and the power to appreciate it in others. Whistler admired Mrs. Leyland and when she was in London, and her husband was in Liverpool, would act as her escort at the opera and elsewhere. She was just the kind of slender, elegant woman to appeal to him, and had she been free he would probably have married her. He became engaged for a while to her youngest sister, but somehow the affair was broken off. The sister was prettier than Mrs. Leyland, but lacked the quick feminine sympathy which Whistler prized more than any other quality in women. Mrs. Leyland sent her butler to help with Whistler's first party at Lindsey Row,

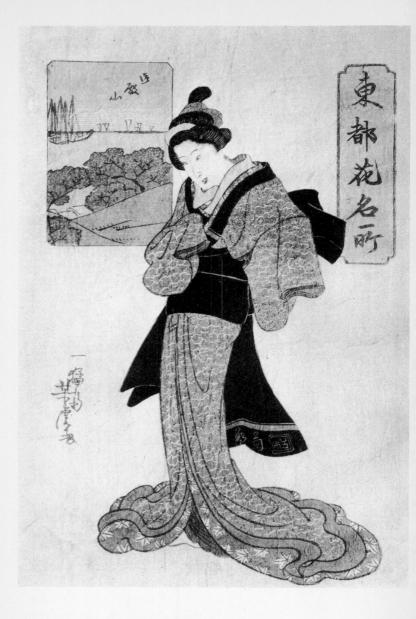

YOSHITORA: *Color woodcut. In the*
*Victoria and Albert Museum.*

LA PRINCESSE DU PAYS DE LA
PORCELAINE: *In the Charles L.
Freer Collection, National Gallery of
American Art.*

and he took great delight in designing the dress—white and rose chiffon adorned with rosettes—in which she was to sit for her portrait. When she was unable to come, Maud posed in the white and rose dress for her, and one cannot help wondering what she thought of the whole matter. Apparently she was not jealous of Mrs. Leyland, but the woman whom Whistler finally married was less accommodating, and when Mrs. Leyland tried, in later years, to bring about a *rapprochement,* upbraided her with attempting to break up the peace of a happy home.

Certainly in the early years of their friendship, Whistler took great pleasure in Mrs. Leyland's company. With his mother he spent long weeks at Speke Hall, near Liverpool, and Leyland commissioned him to paint the portraits of the entire family, generously paying for them beforehand. It is sad to reflect that none was ever finished, unless we except the portrait of Leyland which gave Whistler an infinity of trouble before he could paint the legs to his satisfaction.

Leyland was not satisfied with the possession of a country house near Liverpool, and whether urged thereto by Mrs. Leyland's love of society or by his own ambition, he purchased a London house at 49 Prince's Gate. With the example of the Medici before him, he aspired to be a patron of all the arts, and to fill his house not only with the treasures of the past but with the best productions of his contemporaries.

The exterior of 49 Prince's Gate was in no way distinguished from that of hundreds of other houses in the West End of London. Leyland decided to leave it as it was, but to transform the interior into a kind of Italian palace. It was natural that he should turn for help to Murray Marks, who had helped so many to make their collections and who was glad to do all he could to make the ship-owner's dream come true.

The dealer recommended Norman Shaw as the most suitable architect to transform the interior, and for the details of decoration he proposed a friend of his, Jeckyll, a young man whose considerable talents had not yet been recognized. Leyland was already, by Marks's advice, a collector of "Blue and White" porcelain, and it was decided that Jeckyll should transform the dining-room into a suitable background for its display. Marks also advised Leyland in the choice of his pictures, and it was under his influence that the ship-owner bought seven by Burne-Jones, nine by Rossetti, three by Albert Moore, and one each by Ford Madox Brown and Watts, as well as no fewer than nine by Botticelli.

The visitor found himself first in a large entrance hall, and was struck at once by the wide staircase, splendid with a gilt-bronze balustrade saved from the demolition of Northumberland House. On the pillar from which the balustrade sprang stood a statuary group from the prow of a Venetian galley—two female figures of gilded wood, one

seated and one waving an oriflamme. On the mosaic floor
was spread a profusion of oriental rugs, and a large screen
stood against the wall as a background for enormous vases
of cloisonné enamel interspersed with gilt Italian chairs.
In the center, as a concession to comfort, was a large and
heavily upholstered divan in the taste of the seventies. On
the walls hung Rossetti's "Loving-Cup," "Sea Spell," "Dis
Manibus" and "La Pia," Burne-Jones's "Circe" and "Cupid
Reviving Psyche," and the portrait of Rossetti by Watts to
serve as an image of the presiding deity.

We must borrow the pen of an enthusiastic visitor to
describe the rest of the mansion: [1]

> The morning-room is exceedingly cozy and com-
> fortable, and at the same time every object in it is in
> good taste. The walls and ceilings are paneled with
> oak, inlaid with black and white woods in a simple
> geometrical design. The walls above the dado are
> covered with three large and six smaller pieces of
> Beauvais tapestry, with Teniers subjects, in perfect
> preservation and freshness of color. On the floor is a
> bright oriental carpet. The cabinets are of Indian,
> Tyrolese, and Italian work beautifully inlaid. The
> bibelots and ornaments are all choice, but discreetly
> arranged.
>
> Down a few steps . . . we find ourselves in the
> merchant's sanctum, a long room paneled with Amer-

[1] See "A Pre-Raphaelite Mansion," by Theodore Child, Harper's Magazine, December, 1890, p. 81.

ican walnut and hung above the dado with old-gold Spanish leather. The furniture of the room is completed by inlaid cabinets of German and Italian origin, Chippendale chairs, modern easy chairs, a grand piano, a Louis XVI bureau, and an Italian *cassone* or marriage coffer.

Three "ideal women" by Albert Moore stand at the top of the stairs, and beyond is a vast salon divided into three by huge screens of paneled and carved walnut with bars of burnished brass, suggested to Norman Shaw by the roodloft of the cathedral of Bar-le-Duc. "The furniture is composed of divans, chairs, inlaid Indo-Portuguese cabinets and a harpsichord by Ruckers, with a finely painted and lacquered case, a grand piano, incrusted Boule cabinets, an elegant chest of drawers by Riesener . . . ," Venetian mirrors, Milanese tables, Portuguese hangings, Renaissance bronzes, oriental vases, Rossetti's "Blessed Damozel," Burne-Jones's "Merlin and Viviane," a Botticelli Madonna, an "Adoration of the Magi" by Lippo Lippi, curtains of cherry-red Genoa velvet on cloth of gold, and a carved wood overmantel designed by Norman Shaw.

The dining-room was entrusted to Jeckyll. It occupied all his thoughts; his reputation as a decorator was to be founded upon it. He erected new walls, he paneled the ceiling, the pendent eaves terminating in gas-lamps, and added here and there to the dark wood a discreet touch of gold. For the walls he procured, at a cost of one thousand pounds, a quantity of old Spanish leather which had hung for three hundred years or more in a house in Norfolk. This was historic leather brought to England by Catherine of Aragon, and displaying her device of the open pomegranate and a series of small richly colored flowers.[2] A rug with a red border was placed upon the floor and the "Blue and White" carefully arranged on the shelves prepared to receive it. Then Whistler's appropriate picture "La Princesse du Pays de la Porcelaine" was hoisted into position over the mantelpiece, and Leyland's dining-room was complete.

But by the placing of that picture the whole creation was to be shattered. A serpent had entered into the Pre-Raphaelite Eden. Whistler, curiously enough, had already been employed in the decoration of the house and had painted for the staircase a number of "panels imitating aventurine lacquer, decorated with delicate sprigs of pale rose and white flowers in the Japanese taste." But he must have been completely out of sympathy with the overloaded

[2] "It will be remembered that Ferdinand V had just conquered Granada (period 1483-85) when he received news of the birth of his daughter Catherine, and so to commemorate the great victory, and the birth of his daughter, he gave to her as her badge the Granada or pomegranate, and this was adopted and exhibited as her badge and symbol. It appeared extensively in the leather at Mr. Leyland's house, and therefore, in all probability, these hangings of leather were part of the furnishing which were presented to Queen Catherine by the City of Cordova and brought over by her at the time of her arriving as the bride for Prince Arthur and afterwards for Henry VIII."—Dr. G. C. Williamson in "Murray Marks and His Friends" (London, 1919).

style adopted throughout the house. His ideal of decoration was a plain wall with two pictures, both by Whistler.

He was pleased that his "Princesse" had been given the place of honor in the dining-room. The picture was most appropriate; it was the setting that needed a little altering. He complained to Leyland that the red flowers in the Spanish leather "killed" the pale tones of the "Princesse." Leyland, anxious for peace, but without consulting Jeckyll, allowed Whistler to experiment, and the latter began by cutting the red border from the rug and painting the red flowers gold. The result was horrible, as even Whistler was constrained to admit. The gold flowers and the color of the leather clashed; Whistler proceeded to remedy this by painting out the leather.

He had once drawn up a scheme for a previous client who had rejected it. This scheme, of which only a few slight pen-drawings yet existed, was based on the motif of peacocks' feathers, and no doubt derived ultimately from some oriental painting Whistler had seen. Whistler promised Leyland that he would restore harmony in the room, and he painted a small corner of the leather to show what he meant to do. As the season was over, the Leylands left London. Whistler was left alone in the huge dining-room with his own picture, his own ideas on decoration, and another man's handiwork. There was only one way to make harmony: the other man's work must be destroyed.

He was filled with a furious energy, and, calling his

assistants together, he proceeded to remold Leyland's dining-room nearer to his heart's desire. Expensive leather, especially when chosen by another artist, was a delightful surface to work on. It tempted him; he could not keep his brushes away from it. Gradually the flamboyant peacocks spread over the whole room, and clouds of peacocks' feathers flew up to the ceiling and settled there. Even the shutters glittered with blue and gold. Whistler had never worked so hard in his life. Early in the morning his hansom was on its way to Prince's Gate and he was still at the house when night fell, blue paint on his hands and gold leaf in his hair. It was his first chance (and it proved to be his last) of decoration on a grand scale.

Gradually walls, woodwork and ceiling were entirely covered, with the exception of the wall opposite Whistler's picture. The framework was lacquered and clouded, and the panels filled in with feathers. The panels to the right and left of the windows showed peacocks with their tails spread, advancing in perspective one behind the other, the birds in gold and the ground in blue. On the middle panel were two peacocks with pendent tails sweeping the ground. Whistler planned to have a carpet of turquoise-blue and the fireplace inlaid with turquoise-blue mosaic.

Leyland cannot have been entirely unaware of what was afoot. He kept urging Whistler to finish, but the artist still worked on. Leyland was busy and unable to get to London. He was used to the ways of artists and thought that he might as well let things take their course. Even when Whistler hinted that the cost might be heavy, Leyland was not perturbed; he had plenty of money.

Soon, however, rumors begin to reach him, rumors of incredible happenings in his new house. Whistler is getting out of hand completely. Wherever he goes he talks of nothing but the Peacock Room and invites everyone to come and see it. "Everyone" goes.

Fashionable strollers, finding themselves in the neighborhood of Prince's Gate, say to one another, "Let's go and see the Peacock Room." They enter Leyland's house and are shown into a grotto gleaming with blue and gold. Whistler, uttering shrill cries, runs down his ladder to shake them by the hand. He seems half crazy with enthusiasm. "I am doing the loveliest thing you ever saw!"

Royalty enters in the person of the Duke of Teck and Princess Louise; old friends look in—ladies he has known in his dancing days—and he dances with them amid the paint-pots; newspaper men arrive and are given a printed leaflet explaining the decorations, so that there shall be no mistake. Old Sir Henry Cole strolls over from the museum and tells Whistler that his work is as careful as Mulready's. Whistler spits fire. Still people arrive; the talk becomes more animated. Whistler is holding a reception.

Unnoticed, a furtive figure creeps into the room. It is Jeckyll, who has heard the rumors and come to see for himself. He looks for the warm brown tone of his beautiful leather; blue shrieks at him from every corner of the room; the gold blinds him; peacocks' eyes follow him; and from the midst of the crowd the "strident peacock laugh" of the man who has committed this outrage. The shock cracks his brain. He staggers home and is found a few hours later muttering to himself and trying to cover the floor of his room with gold. He dies in a madhouse.

Mrs. Leyland, unexpected in London, lets herself into her own house with a private key. From the dining-room comes a babel of voices. Unseen, she slips into the room. In the group surrounding Whistler someone asks: "Does Leyland know? Have you consulted him?"

"Why should I? I am doing the most beautiful thing that ever has been done."

Something inaudible follows, and then, in Whistler's piercing voice, heard all over the house: "Well! What can you expect from a *parvenu?*"

Even Whistler's most fervid partizans are constrained to admit that Leyland behaved very well in the whole affair. He did not care very much for the decorations when they were done, and he thought (quite rightly) that blue and gold is not the best setting for blue china. Certainly the "Blue and White" pots were as completely killed by Whistler's peacocks as Whistler's "Princesse" had been killed by Jeckyll's leather. Moreover, the leather had cost one thousand pounds. But what irritated him most was the way in which his house had been turned into a combined picture gallery and salon for Whistler's friends. In particular he resented the leaflet given to the press, and all the subsequent publicity. He felt indeed that he had been made to look rather foolish by being shouldered out of his own house by the man he had employed to decorate it.

He asked Whistler how much he considered his work was worth, and Whistler answered, "Two thousand guineas." Leyland thought the sum excessive, and so did Rossetti, who was consulted by Leyland in the matter. In the end Leyland offered Whistler a thousand pounds, and Whistler, with a very bad grace, accepted it. It irked him, especially, that Leyland had "knocked off his shillings," as he called paying in pounds instead of guineas. Whistler was a little mad on the subject of guineas. To him the difference between a pound and a guinea was not the difference between twenty shillings and twenty-one, but the difference between being treated as a tradesman and treated as a professional man or an artist. Such a feeling is very English and almost impossible to explain to a foreigner, but Whistler had absorbed it as completely as if his first knickerbockers had been ordered in Savile Row and paid for in guineas. A thousand guineas for his work might have sent him away not too dissatisfied, but a thousand pounds seemed to him a deliberate insult.

Leyland was very willing that the room should be left as it was, but Whistler insisted on finishing it. He had seen his opportunity for revenge. So on the wall opposite to where his own picture hung, the wall which Leyland would see as he dined at the head of his table, Whistler painted two superb peacocks, and under the claw of one of them was a pile of coins. Leyland, to his permanent credit, did not touch a line of it.

Whistler had lost his most generous patron, and afterwards admitted that he had "never had any luck" since the Peacock Room. For the moment, however, this was hardly apparent. Sitters were not lacking. The decade of the seventies was a period of unexampled prosperity for the English upper middle classes, indeed for the upper classes generally. Taxation was low, the National Debt was negligible, and there were as yet very few of the social services that are now such a heavy burden on the national exchequer. A great many modern luxuries had not yet been invented, and the successful business man had money to spend on pictures which he would now spend in more sporting or more mechanical fashion. It was a golden age for the conventional artist.

Very few of the well-to-do lived in small apartments. The large house was the rule. The modern taste for austerity in decoration was unthought of. Immense drawing-rooms needed a multitude of chairs, a profusion of knick-knacks, palms for every corner and pictures for every wall. A fortune was awaiting the academic painter who knew how to cover a sufficient area of canvas with the politely

sentimental or the discreetly erotic. Edwin Long's "Baby-
lonian Marriage Market" has become almost the classical
example of the taste of the period. It was bought in 1875
for £1,700 and changed hands seven years later for the
astounding sum of £6,615.

The teacups of Queen's Gate and Bayswater clinked
to the sound of animated conversations on the theme of
Art. Art, like politics, was a subject with which men and
women of the world were permitted to concern themselves.
The Academy was taken as seriously as the House of Commons, and the rival merits of Poynter and Leader, of
Herkomer, of Leighton himself and the now tamed
Millais, were disputed by eager young men and women less
frankly barbarian than they have since become. A few
bolder voices around the conventional tea-tables suggested
that Whistler and Burne-Jones might one day be received
into the bosom of the Academy. In more advanced circles
the Academy was already losing its prestige. The Esthetic
Movement had begun.

It is a curious commentary on English manners that in
England esthetic movements almost always assume a social
flavor as soon as they begin to have any success at all. But
snobbery is slow-witted, and so the first wave of any movement foams away ineffectually, except in so far as it
awakens public interest and informs the more or less fashionable world that something is afoot. The first wave slides
back defeated; it is the second that rolls on to victory.

So it was with Pre-Raphaelitism and its successor, the Esthetic Movement.

By the later seventies Pre-Raphaelitism, which had never been more than a loose association of painters with different aims, had fallen to pieces. In the public view, Rossetti *was* Pre-Raphaelitism, and Rossetti himself was breaking up. Insomnia and the chloral he took to overcome it had undermined what must have been a singularly strong constitution. The melancholy that had haunted him ever since his wife's death was now ever-present. His mind was clouded with suspicion. The attacks of Robert Buchanan, although repelled by Rossetti's friends, had eaten deeply into his mind. He saw enemies everywhere. He imagined, quite falsely, that the greater part of the public was bitterly hostile to him and to his work. When he was approached with a request to exhibit in the Grosvenor Gallery—the new venture which should have set the seal upon his fame —he refused, and the laurels which might have been his were gathered by Burne-Jones. This was unfortunate both for Rossetti and for the Grosvenor Gallery. As Mr. Evelyn Waugh remarks in his book on Rossetti: "Without him or Madox Brown the Gallery broke, instead of carrying on, the tradition of the Pre-Raphaelites. Burne-Jones swam into instant fame, and from the first set the tone of the annual exhibitions. If the robust influence of Madox Brown and Rossetti had been given full scope, English art might easily have escaped from the 'greenery-yallery fever.'"

English art did not so escape, and the strange disease, and Whistler's part in it, must be briefly considered.

The Esthetic Movement is one of the most curious and complicated phenomena of English social history. The continued popularity of the works of Gilbert and Sullivan, including "Patience," has preserved a set of attitudes that would otherwise have vanished from the world, except of course from Oxford. Oxford has a way of preserving these relics of a lost cause, especially when such a cause is partly at least her own child.

Bunthorne is the Esthete of the eighties looked at through hostile eyes, and because those eyes were Gilbert's, the figure that he saw still lives in popular estimation. But other contemporaries saw him too, the frail, wilting youth with the poppy or the lily in his medieval hand. Jokes about young men contemplating lilies in lieu of luncheon occur in Punch as early as 1880, and a year earlier there are references to "Passionate Brompton," the inhabitants of which were in the habit of asking one another such a question as, "Are you intense?" or discoursing upon High Art with "a certain hungry look of ineffable yearning toward the Infinite."

During this period Punch, than which there is no more accurate reflection of the opinions and prejudices of the more philistine of the British upper middle classes, devoted a considerable portion of its space every week to ridicule of the Esthetes. The master of the revels was Du Maurier.

When Du Maurier inserted his unflattering portrait of Whistler into the first version of "Trilby," Pennell declares that Whistler was painfully surprised at this wanton coup de grâce to old friendship. Whistler was certainly indignant, but it is unlikely that he could have been surprised, for Du Maurier had been indulging in pin-pricks for years, with cause or without. Du Maurier was too closely associated with Punch not to be aware that its attitude to Whistler was consistently hostile. "Mr. James Whistler has created quite a sensation this year in the Grosvenor. Everyone is talking of his great work, 'The Invisible Girl, or Absence Makes the Heart Grow Fonder.'" One of his pictures was caricatured under the title: "Keep it Dark, or The Ghost in the Haunted Coalhole." Such comments could not escape so persistent a reader of press-cuttings.

Punch, however, showed a certain obtuseness in connecting Whistler so closely with the Esthetic Movement. The Esthetes adored Blue China, and Whistler had been one of the first to collect it. But it was because he had infected Rossetti with the craze that it became part of the Esthetic tradition. The Esthetes had palpitations before anything Japanese, but again Whistler had been responsible only through Rossetti. His own *crise de Japonisme* was over long before, except for the throwback of the Peacock Room.

In Estheticism, the oriental impulses were mingled with a medievalism with which Whistler had nothing to

[ 167 ]

do. That was the work of the Pre-Raphaelites, and between them and Whistler there was a great gulf fixed. With the other threads of this extremely complex cloth he had even less connection. The Esthetes, especially the women, wore "reformed clothes"—loose, blouselike garments of indeterminate cut and color. Whistler was as much obsessed by elegance as a man-milliner. With the exception of the early "White Girl," all his women give the impression of being tightly laced. In the later development of Estheticism there was a morbid streak which was quite foreign to his nature. Whistler was about as morbid as a colonel of cavalry.

Punch, however, was too busy ridiculing the whole movement to take note of such fine distinctions. Whistler was much in the company of Wilde; Swinburne had written poems on his pictures. That was enough for the caricaturists.

Du Maurier was already, in a different medium, displaying his talents as a novelist. His characters were not the mere figurants of a single cartoon. They reappeared week by week. They developed their eccentricities, they rose in the world, they became as real to the readers of Punch as the characters in Dickens. There was Mrs. Cimabue Brown, there was Mrs. Lyon Hunter (later refined to Mrs. Leo Hunter); there was Prigsby, the critic, Maundle, the painter, and Jellaby Postlethwaite, the Esthetic poet. They lived in a world of dadoes, of artistic wallpaper (it was a shock to Punch that wall-paper *could* be

[ 168 ]

"artistic"), of brass fenders, of Japanese fans and bunches of lilies in blue pots. They thought the paintings of Burne-Jones "consummately precious" and "quite too utter." (It is amusing to note, in this connection, that while the use, or abuse, of the word "precious" can be traced back to Ruskin, the word itself has now become permanently colored by its connection with the Esthetic Movement.)

One would have expected the Esthetic Movement, in one of its aspects at least, to be more in tune with Ruskin's ideals than was Pre-Raphaelitism. For Rossetti's art, in spite of his teaching at the Working Men's College, was essentially a turning away from the sordidness of an industrial age into the twilight of the imagination. His was no attempt to reform the age, an end to which Ruskin devoted all the heavy artillery of his passionate eloquence. But on the crest of the second wave—the early Esthetic Movement —rode William Morris and Burne-Jones, and the former, at least, regarded the Middle Ages not as a dreamer's paradise but as a practical ideal. With his own hands he carpentered, dyed stuffs, printed books, and, in order that his works might reach the public, founded the firm (of artist-decorators as they would now be called) of Morris, Marshall, Faulkner and Company.

Ruskin's dream of the beautifying of every English home was not realized. How should it be? The artist cannot compete with the machine in supplying the poor with the articles they need. Morris's goods were expensive, sometimes extremely so, and, whatever their ultimate influence, their first effect was to provide a handful of the sophisticated rich with a new snobbery, a new superiority to the vulgar herd.

The result was the rise of a cult, a body of adepts who turned the new gospel into a personal decoration, so that while Ruskin turned more and more to Socialism, the Esthetic Movement dwindled into the doctrine of Art for Art's sake. This attitude was very nearly Whistler's own, but with a significant difference. As Whistler had never professed any moral purpose in his art, he was never driven to repudiate it. The later Esthetes spent most of their time repudiating moral purpose. Their anxiety to clear themselves of the taint of "uplift" and philanthropy led them to behave with the self-conscious extravagance of a vicar's daughter at a night-club. It is very difficult for England to breed the true bohemian. Moral values are too deeply rooted. Whistler had absorbed the French point of view in these matters, and although he was not, in the true sense, a bohemian either, it was not conscience but code that saved him, not religion but "West Point."

He stands out, therefore, from those whom it pleased Punch to confound with him, because his eccentricity of attire and conduct was personal and egotistical, instead of social and fashionable. He never wilted, he never drooped, he never descended to soul-culture, and although the public might class him with the Esthetes, the Esthetes knew better, for some of them had already suffered at his hands. Hence when the Grosvenor Gallery hurled Whistler into his fight with Ruskin, the recognized leaders of Estheticism were found on Ruskin's side. For Estheticism had a certain esprit de corps from which Whistler was excluded.

Behind all the posing and posturing of the "utterly utter" there was, in the minds of a few enlightened patrons of art, a genuine desire to give the younger painters a chance. So the Esthetic Movement found both its justification and its social apotheosis in the opening of the Grosvenor Gallery in 1877. No more was the Academy to be the only doorway to fame. No more were its decrees to be accepted as absolute by the cultivated people of London. The Grosvenor Gallery was to inaugurate a new epoch. It did.

Sir Coutts Lindsay was a wealthy banker and a man of taste. His house at 5 Cromwell Place, later to be the residence of Sir John Lavery, had—what was rare in those days—a studio, and the ceiling of the studio was a blue firmament powdered all over with stars. He decided that something most be done to rescue English taste from the lethargy into which it seemed to have fallen, and he, with several others, conceived the idea of financing a gallery of modern art. Charles Hallé, the artist (son of Sir Charles Hallé, the pianist), was one of his two chief supporters, and the other was a critic on the staff of the Westminster Review, a brilliant young man named Comyns Carr. Mrs.

Comyns Carr was herself a valiant supporter of the Esthetic Movement, wore loose esthetic gowns, and is generally understood to have been the original of Du Maurier's Cimabue Brown. With Comyns Carr's critical support, with Sir Coutts Lindsay's financial backing, and with the social prestige imparted to the enterprise by Lady Lindsay's aristocratic friends, the projected gallery seemed to have more than a fair chance of success.

The gallery was conveniently situated for the carriages of Mayfair. The furnishing and appointments were luxurious. The principal room had been transformed into the likeness of an Italian palace, the walls hung with old red damask and green velvet, and the ceiling a replica of Sir Coutts Lindsay's own. Comyns Carr's knowledge of the world of artists was made use of in order to insure a representative collection of canvases, especially from those who could not, or would not, exhibit at the Royal Academy.

Fortune, or the wisdom of Sir Coutts Lindsay, had provided a restaurant on the premises, underneath the room where the pictures were shown, and at the opening there was a banquet, honored by the presence of the Prince and Princess of Wales. The Academy itself could not have mustered a more distinguished company, but the space in the restaurant was limited, and so, to mitigate the disappointment of those who had not been invited, an enormous reception was held in the very room where the pictures were shown. The tactics of the banker were entirely successful. The opening of the Grosvenor Gallery was the event of the season. Whistler was entirely at home in such surroundings, and became a more conspicuous figure than ever. His pictures, however, did not attract the attention he had hoped for. They were "killed" by the too luxurious surroundings, and, unfortunately, Whistler could not transform the Grosvenor Gallery as he had transformed Leyland's house.

He had a genuine excusable hatred of the museum style of house decoration, and yet it remained the ideal even of the most cultivated of his contemporaries. Morris and his friends, with all their love of beauty, had only succeeded in cluttering the houses of their patrons with more bric-à-brac, medieval instead of mid-Victorian. When would they learn the lesson of Japanese simplicity and appropriateness? Whistler had introduced them to Japanese art, and all they had done with it was to mass it in heaps on the top of their already crowded cabinets and sideboards. Whistler knew of the enormous sums which Leyland had lavished on Prince's Gate. With a hundredth part of the money he could, he knew, have built the perfect house, or at least directed its building and decorated it when it was finished.

There was perhaps only one man in London in sympathy with his ideals. E. W. Godwin was an architect by profession, but he was also interested in the stage, and has had considerable influence on theatrical costume. He found scope for his enthusiasm in organizing private theatricals, and Whistler may have met him at some social functions of the kind. He was married to a pretty woman, the daughter of Philip, the sculptor, but his amours were notorious, and among his friends he was known as "the wicked Earl." Handsome, enthusiastic, and unconventional, he attracted Whistler, and when the two men found that they showed a common taste in decoration, they became close friends. After one of their discussions on architecture, it was decided that Godwin should build a house for Whistler.

Whistler's extravagance was as great as ever, and his receipts had begun to show signs of diminishing. Ruskin's attack on his work at the Grosvenor Gallery must, with all its consequences, be left to the next chapter, but its immediate effect was to make Whistler's pictures harder to sell. If, therefore, he resolved to move into a larger house and to have the house built for him by Godwin, it was not because he was more prosperous than he had been, but because he intended to turn the place into a source of profit. In a word, he intended to start a school.

Artists born in the nineteenth century were, in one way at least, unfortunate, for perhaps for the first time in the history of painting they found themselves without a tradition. This lack of a tradition, of an accepted manner of working, is what renders the study of nineteenth-century art so profoundly confusing. The student was no longer

[ 174 ]

brought up from boyhood in personal intimacy with an established painter, grinding his colors, filling in his backgrounds, and finally graduating to the position of an independent artist. Instead, he found himself a member of an "academy" where the teaching was fragmentary and inconclusive. Even the *atelier* of Gleyre had not been a master's studio in the old sense of the term, and Whistler was conscious of how little he had learned there and how much time he had wasted before finding his own manner. Whistler himself had no very complete system to impart, but of this he could hardly be expected to be aware.

At the back of his mind there was always the notion that one day he should be able to *faire école*. He toyed with the idea of imparting his principles to others, of raising disciples to fight his battles, and of discomfiting his enemies by becoming an influence as well as a phenomenon. His studios had always been small as he scorned the conventional sky-light, preferring the light which came from an ordinary window, sometimes through a half-drawn blind. At No. 2 Lindsey Row he had sufficient space for his own needs, but he saw that larger premises would be needed if he intended to found a school.

Godwin drew up his plans, a site was chosen in Tite Street, Chelsea, estimates were accepted and building operations commenced. The result was the famous "White House." The walls were of white brick, the roof of green slate, the whole design (in an age of Gothic doorways,

[ 175 ]

Dutch gables, and Scottish baronial skylines) suspiciously plain, indeed, so plain that the local authorities insisted on some decorative moldings being added in order to keep up the "tone" of the neighborhood. Once more Whistler's taste was thirty years in advance of that of his contemporaries. He took possession of his house in October, 1878. Six months later he was declared bankrupt. The Ruskin libel action had ruined him.

## CHAPTER VII

### THE POT OF PAINT

IN the year 1868 the English art world was startled by a munificent and entirely unexpected gift. Felix Slade, a wealthy proctor in Doctors' Commons, had, throughout his life, been a great admirer and collector of works of art, and at his death he bequeathed thirty-five thousand pounds for the endowment of professorships in fine art at the universities of Oxford and Cambridge, and in University College, London. The gift to London has given rise to one of the most famous schools of art in the world—the Slade School—but it is with the consequences of his gift to Oxford that we are most concerned here.

Oxford, for many reasons, was not a very suitable place for the setting-up of an art school in the usual sense. Artists are rarely drawn from the classes of society that still form the majority of undergraduates at the older universities. The authorities even yet have not included a course in the fine arts among the subjects set for examination, and there is no English equivalent of the German *Kunstforscher*. The chair endowed by Slade at Oxford is, therefore, a kind of pulpit, the prestige of which depends almost entirely on the preacher. When it was first founded it was essential

[ 177 ]

to find someone who already had the public ear in art matters, someone whose reputation would make the chair rather than need to be made by it.

There was one man, above all others, who seemed destined for the post: the "Graduate of Oxford" who had written "Modern Painters," who had constituted himself the champion of Turner and had created the vogue of the Pre-Raphaelites.

John Ruskin was then a man of fifty. He was born on February 8, 1819, and had devoted the whole of his industrious life to the study of art and to the publication of his opinions. Of his sincerity, of his knowledge, and of his literary power there could be no question. Other candidates for the Slade chair were put forward, but it was obvious from the first that Ruskin would be chosen. The official invitation sent to him was unanimous in asking him to accept the post.

Ruskin was abroad when he received the message. He recognized its importance, and was grateful for the official acknowledgment of a position that he had reached by his own efforts. Years before he had urged the establishment of just such a chair, and now he was called upon to occupy it himself. He hurried home to take up his first professorship.

The years 1870 to 1878 were to be the busiest years of his busy life. He threw himself into his duties with the energy of a man who had no distractions. Yet he had many, for he had already emerged from the stage when he was content to study art and let the world go on as best it could. It may be doubted whether such an attitude had ever detained him.

Ruskin was, by nature, a profoundly religious man, even when his doubts of conventional religion were most powerful. His early training—for his parents had dedicated him to the Church almost at birth—had left a deep mark on his character. "Art for Art's sake" seemed to him mere impiety, and Whistler's belief that the artist should content himself with doing his job, mere selfishness. The very passion of his interest in art caused him great uneasiness of conscience. The Puritan in him was very strong, and (as A. C. Benson once pointed out) he came of Lowland Scottish stock, a soil fertile in prophets. Had not Carlyle himself sprung from the same?

In 1870 he was already deep in sociological problems. He saw truly enough, in spite of Whistler's favorite doctrine, that the artist is not and cannot be divorced from his environment, that easel-painting—"high art," as it was called—cannot flourish in a world which allows the applied arts to decay. For him, at least, there was no peace in "the Palace of Art" while beggars starved at its doors. He felt that he had no right to enjoy the triumphs of painting while the ravages of industrialism turned the face of England black. It was because he cared so much for beauty that he set out to reform the world.

[ 179 ]

A man must be strangely insensitive not to feel the pathos and the heroism of that unequal struggle, and the modern world owes to Ruskin in many departments of life more than it is always ready to admit. He set out to move a mountain, and he did move it, even if ever so little. Is it to be wondered at that he scarred his hands and spoiled his temper in the process?

How he performed a tithe of the tasks he set himself is a mystery. During his Oxford professorship, social reform became an obsession with him. He tried to improve the taste of the masses by starting a cheap library of standard literature. Where books were lacking—on botany, geology, drawing—he wrote them himself. He founded a museum at Sheffield; he organized his "St. George's Guild," a new order of chivalry, and gave a tenth of his fortune to its fund. He kept up an extensive correspondence; he wrote regularly to the newspapers to denounce current evils and suggest remedies, and every month he published "Fors Clavigera," a personal address to all who would listen, a kind of pastoral letter of exhortation and remonstrance, an incessant clarion call for the regeneration of the world. One would have to go back a hundred years, to the career of Wesley, to find a parallel for such tireless activity for the betterment of mankind.

During those years he can hardly ever have stopped writing. In 1875 he had seven large books in the press at once. We may forgive such a man a certain impatience with the selfishness and laziness of others. Unfortunately, the picture has its other side. Ruskin's taste was uncertain, and his system of esthetics—if system it can be called—wholly erroneous. When a picture pleased him, he praised it for its "truth to nature," and seemed to think that the greatness of an artist could be explained in terms of his knowledge of plant-form. He was obsessed by "beauty of subject" and so could see no virtue in the great Dutchmen, not even in Rembrandt. Also, he suffered from the pet vice of prophets—a belief in their own infallibility. "I'm not arguing with you, I'm telling you," was Whistler's phrase, but it perfectly describes Ruskin's attitude.

Of the esthetic revolution which was happening in France he was wholly unconscious, but we may be sure that if he had known anything of the work of Manet he would have disliked it as much as Rossetti did. Whistler's painting could scarcely fail to attract his notice, and he detested it. The passage in "Fors Clavigera" which Whistler thought libelous was not the first time he had expressed his opinion of that artist's work. As early as 1873, in the third lecture on Tuscan art which he delivered in Oxford, he said: "I never saw anything so impudent on the walls of any exhibition in any country as last year in London. It was a daub, professing to be 'a harmony in pink and white' (or some such nonsense); absolute rubbish, and which had taken about a quarter of an hour to scrawl or daub—it had no pretense to be called painting. The price asked was two hundred and fifty guineas."

It is interesting to note in this passage all the elements

[ 181 ]

of the later libel. The use of the word "impudent," as if
the painting of a picture not in accordance with the critic's
rules were a personal insult; the unfairness of the distorted
title, "a harmony in pink and white," when the picture
criticized must have been one of three exhibited in 1872
in the Winter Exhibition of Cabinet Pictures in Oil at the
Dudley Gallery: "Symphony in Gray and Green," "Nocturne in Gray and Gold," or "Nocturne in Blue and
Silver"; the harping on the price, and the implied accusation of dishonesty in charging so much for a picture so
"unfinished." All that is lacking is the name of the artist.
Four years later, when Ruskin came to repeat the passage
in different words, he repaired the omission, and Whistler
sued him.

In "Fors Clavigera" Ruskin shed the intricacy and formality of his style, and strove to write as naturally and
simply as possible in order that his message might be understood by everybody. In consequence the book into which
the series grew is the most personal of all his works. It is
vivid, rambling, distressingly revealing. He makes no secret
of his faults and none of his virtues. Even his openhanded-
ness with money is faithfully reported, not in order that
others should admire him but that they should go and do
likewise. It is both the rich outpouring of a noble mind and
the painful exposure of a good man's foibles. Cardinal
Manning said that it was like the beating of one's heart in
a nightmare.

Ruskin had never lacked courage. He attacked Claude in his first book and he strongly criticized Michelangelo in the very precincts of the University Museum at Oxford. In "Fors Clavigera" he cast aside all restraint, and as the seventies wore on and the pressure of overwork grew greater, he became steadily more and more violent.

In judging Ruskin's attack on Whistler, it is only fair to remember that it came from a man who was well on his way to brain-fever. But it was not only the burden of his work which tended to throw him off his balance. The troubles of his early domestic life are well known and need not be set down here, but in the early seventies he had begun to hope that after all his life was not to be as loveless as he feared. The object of his affections was a delicate, beautiful creature named Rose La Touche. Ruskin made proposals to her, but Rose, who was a strict Evangelical, rejected him on account of what she considered the looseness of his faith. Ruskin recognized the force of her objections and was much disheartened by them, and when Rose La Touche died in May, 1875, the wound bled afresh. Ruskin's friends thought it would be better for him to obtain a year's leave of absence from his professorship and go abroad. He took their advice, and it was natural that he should make his way to Venice.

He had, of course, been there before, but he saw many changes. When he had visited it in the fifties it was still under Austrian domination, and Marmont, Duke of Ragusa, last of the Napoleonic marshals, could still be met at tea-parties. Twenty years later such links with the past had been snapped. The white coats of the Austrian officers had disappeared from the great Piazza, and an Italian architect was busy restoring St. Mark's.

Ruskin had gone to Venice to rest, but so gross a challenge to his principles could not pass unnoticed, and he resolved to compel the authorities to leave St. Mark's alone. He was already well known in Venice, and his friends welcomed him gladly. Clad in an ill-fitting dark blue frock coat with high cravat and collar, he sped from one to another, striving to interest them all in his projects. He made the acquaintance of a young man who was as much concerned with preventing the vandalism of restorers as he was himself. The society of this young man gave him immense pleasure, for he was not only Ruskin's disciple but a member of the patrician house of Morosini, and no one was more conscious than Ruskin of the glamor surrounding the very names of the old Venetian nobility. Morosini published a pamphlet, of which Ruskin wrote the preface, and the restorations of St. Mark's were happily stayed.

Ruskin had come to Venice to rest, but how could anyone gifted with imagination rest in Venice, especially one to whom Venetian painting was a revelation? His mind was bathed in a golden glow, shot with the colors of the masters of the Scuolo di San Rocco. Ruskin never forgot the present; it was to him a perpetual weight upon

[ 184 ]

his conscience, an added burden upon an already overladen mind, but in Venice he could, for a moment at least, put it aside and see before the eye of his imagination an endless pageant of doges and senators, of symbolic and Olympian women, of churches and campaniles and princely houses, stretching away on either side of a canal like a street in paradise, leading onward into the eye of the sun. A semi-mystical element began to enter more and more into these contemplations, and against the gorgeous background of the Adriatic city stood out with unearthly clearness the frail figure of St. Ursula, for whom Ruskin was developing a veritable cult.

It is difficult without a still greater straining of language to convey to the reader all that Venice meant to him, and it is one of the ironies of esthetic history that the state of mind which his residence there induced was the direct cause of sending to his favorite city the artist for whose work he had the least affection, and who was to see his canals and plazas with such different eyes.

The effect of his activities abroad was to send him back to England even more overwrought than when he had set out. The contrast between the beauty of the past and the hideousness of the industrial present revolted him more than ever. The voice of the prophet became more querulous; the temper of the reformer more uncertain. He plunged once more into his manifold activities for the regeneration of England.

[ 185 ]

He returned from the Continent in June, 1876, and before a month was out was more unwell than ever. We find him complaining in his diary of giddiness and dizziness, the preludes to the mental storm which was soon to overwhelm him. He spent his time partly at Brantwood (writing, writing!) and partly at Oxford, lecturing. He made a hurried journey to London to speak at a meeting of the Society for Prevention of Cruelty to Animals, and while in town it was inevitable that he should go to the first exhibition of the Grosvenor Gallery.

That the gallery was possible at all was, indirectly, his own doing, and, as we have seen, it served to consecrate the fame of his favorite modern artist, Burne-Jones. But Ruskin was not altogether pleased with what he found on its walls. He resolved to devote a number of "Fors Clavigera" to saying exactly what he thought about it.

Even those who are willing to make every allowance for the state of Ruskin's mind at the time must admit that the tone of the whole letter is intolerable. Sir Coutts Lindsay is treated with pompous condescension as "at present an amateur, both in art and shopkeeping," and solemnly warned that "he must take up either one or other business if he would prosper in either." He was also taken to task for including some of his own works, and fault was found with the upholstery and decoration of the gallery. Ruskin criticized severely the way the pictures had been hung, and indeed had not a good word to say for anything until he

[ 186 ]

came to enlarge on the paintings of Burne-Jones. "I *know* that these will be immortal."

But there were half a dozen pictures which roused him to fury. That fellow Whistler was at it again, hanging his unfinished daubs beside honest workmanlike painting and, worse still, setting fantastic prices on his wares as an added insult to the intelligence of the public.

One wonders if Ruskin noticed the "Carlyle," for that was in the gallery as well as the nocturnes, but even if he had, its low tone, the flat simplicity of the handling, and the complete absence of local color would have prejudiced him against it. "The Nocturne in Blue and Silver" (Battersea Bridge) meant nothing to him at all, and near it was Whistler's crowning offense—a splash of gold against a square of blue, so dark as to be almost black. It was Whistler's attempt to paint the last moments of one of those rockets sent up from Cremorne Gardens which he had seen when looking westward from the Chelsea shore.

"For Mr. Whistler's own sake," wrote Ruskin, "no less than for the protection of the purchaser, Sir Coutts Lindsay ought not to have admitted works into the gallery in which the ill-educated conceit of the artist so nearly approached the aspect of wilful imposture. I have seen and heard much of cockney impudence before now, but never expected to hear a coxcomb ask two hundred guineas for flinging a pot of paint in the public's face."

Whistler and G. H. Boughton were alone in the smok-

[ 187 ]

ing room of the Arts Club when Boughton came across Ruskin's outburst. After some hesitation he showed it to Whistler, who read it and said: "It is the most debased *style* of criticism I have had thrown at me yet."

"Sounds like libel," said Boughton.

"Well—that I shall try to find out," he answered, lit a cigarette, and left at once to take the necessary steps.

Ruskin was at first delighted that anyone had had the effrontery to take up his challenge. The prospect of appearing in court, he wrote to Burne-Jones, was "nuts and nectar" to him. He looked forward to an opportunity of asserting his principles before a wide public and was only afraid that "the fellow" would think better of it. He set about collecting witnesses for the defense.

However, he was not to have the opportunity he longed for, for in February, 1878, the storm which had long been threatening him broke. He was confined to bed with an attack of brain-fever brought on by twenty years of persistent overwork, and for days he was delirious. When he recovered his brain was as clear as ever, but he had to admit his weakness, and when the trial opened not Ruskin himself but his physician journeyed to London to assure the court that his patient could not appear.

Ruskin's absence deprived the trial of its main interest. What might have been a magnificent duel, a combat of elephant and tiger, dwindled into a display of shadow-boxing. Ruskin was compelled to leave the principal task of supporting him to Burne-Jones.

[ 188 ]

Whistler on his part had high hopes of bringing half the distinguished artists in London into the witness box on his behalf, but to his disgust he found many of them curiously shy. To admire his work in private was one thing; to appear in open court against the powerful and outspoken critic quite another. Leighton promised to attend, but was summoned to Windsor to receive his knighthood, on becoming President of the Royal Academy.

The case of Whistler *versus* Ruskin opened on November 25, 1878, in the Exchequer Division before Baron Huddleston and a special jury. Mr. Sergeant Parry and Mr. Petheram appeared for the plaintiff; the attorney-general and Mr. Bowen for Ruskin. Mr. Sergeant Parry's opening consisted of a brief history of Whistler's career and a recital of the passage in "Fors Clavigera" which was alleged to have damaged him. Examined by Mr. Petheram, Whistler made the astonishing statement that he was born in St. Petersburg, but otherwise his evidence was correct enough. His object was to prove that he was an accepted artist, whose paintings had been exhibited at the Royal Academy, and whose etchings were in the British Museum and the royal collection at Windsor Castle; that before Ruskin's criticism he was able to sell the nocturnes, and that afterwards he could not do so.

The attorney-general's object was to show that Whistler was an unsuccessful, eccentric, and lazy artist who "knocked off" nocturnes in a couple of days and then

[ 189 ]

offered them for sale at extravagant prices. Whistler's calmness under the wilfully flippant cross-examination was admirable. He explained his use of the word nocturne, and said that to him a picture was not the imitative delineation of natural objects, but an arrangement of light, form, and color. Today it is difficult to believe that so obvious a remark could have awakened any dissent, but artists as well as critics were still obsessed by that doctrine of "truth to nature," the wide dissemination of which had been Ruskin's greatest disservice to the cause of art.

He freely admitted that the musical terms used in description of his picture were analogies only, and that the actual painting of his works sometimes took him very little time—the nocturne in question, two days. The attorney-general demanded if it was for two days' work that Whistler asked two hundred guineas, and the artist retorted: "No; I ask it for the knowledge of a lifetime."

He was next questioned on the meaning of his "Nocturne in Blue and Silver," the lovely view of Battersea Bridge by moonlight which is now one of the treasures of the National Gallery of British Art, Millbank. It is easy, in retrospect, to be contemptuous of the blindness of judge and jury, but it must be remembered that they were confronted with a work of art constructed on principles of which they had no conception. Baron Huddleston asked if the picture was a "correct representation of Battersea Bridge," and seemed to think that a point had been made against Whistler when the latter replied that he had never intended it to be anything of the kind, that it was simply a moonlight scene. If the eccentricities of modern painting have done nothing else they have certainly cured the public of the belief that good painting involves the meticulous imitation of nature.

The judge next demanded if the figures on the top of the bridge were intended to be people, and Whistler disconcertingly replied: "They are just what you like." Whistler did not have much opportunity of displaying his wit, but he got in one or two palpable hits. "Do you think," said the attorney-general, "that you could make me understand the beauty of that picture?" and Whistler replied that the attempt would be hopeless.

Whistler's witnesses were W. M. Rossetti, who admitted that he did not care for "The Falling Rocket," but thought it was worth two hundred guineas, and Albert Moore, who defended the picture strongly.

Ruskin's witnesses were Burne-Jones, Frith, and Tom Taylor, the art critic of the Times. Burne-Jones, as we may well believe, hated the task, especially as the passage called in question had followed hard upon Ruskin's extravagant commendation of himself. He admitted that "The Falling Rocket" had color and atmosphere, but declared that it lacked detail and composition. The exquisite composition of the painting is the most remarkable thing about it, but it certainly lacks detail, as how should it not? Was it not by definition a night-piece? Burne-Jones declared that it was but another unsuccessful attempt to paint the night, and declared (under pressure) that two hundred guineas was too much to pay for it "when you think of the amount of earnest work done for a smaller sum."

The irrelevant question of "finish" was then introduced, and an early Titian was produced in court to show what finish was. Whistler grew very impatient, but his interest revived when Frith entered the witness box. His evidence was bluff and straightforward. There was a pretty color in the Battersea Bridge nocturne but no suggestion of moonlight. It was not worth two hundred guineas. Tom Taylor, to Whistler's amusement, contented himself with reading press cuttings of his own criticism. The case was over. The jury, considerably puzzled by the whole affair, brought in a verdict for the plaintiff with one farthing damages. Both sides were left to pay their own costs.

Both Ruskin and Whistler were sore and disappointed at the result. Ruskin had already contemplated giving up his professorship on account of his health. At the very beginning of the trial we find him writing to Dean Liddell: "I can't be professor any more." The verdict made him forget the reason for his resignation, and he now wrote that "it is not owing to ill-health that I resign, but because the professorship is a farce if it has no right to condemn as well as praise," and, in another letter: "I cannot hold a chair from which I have no power of expressing judgment without being taxed for it by British Law." He forgot that the passage for which Whistler had sued him did not occur in his Oxford lectures but in "Fors Clavigera." He had escaped paying the thousand pounds damages that Whistler had demanded, but his share of the costs came to three hundred and eighty-five pounds. A subscription list was immediately opened, and every penny was contributed by the public. Whistler also opened a subscription list, but no one supported it, and, as he was a much poorer man than Ruskin, he found himself hard pressed.

Even without the cost of the libel action he would have found himself in difficulties. His plea in court that Ruskin had made it difficult for him to sell his pictures was well founded. Sitters became very rare, as few men or women were willing to be painted by a man who had been held up to general ridicule. His house, like all houses, proved much more expensive than he had expected. Extra charges, which Whistler had not foreseen, swelled the builders' accounts to alarming proportions and, in addition, there had been all the expenses of moving, and the enormous bills which he had allowed to accumulate during the years in Lindsey Row.

In his despair he turned to Howell. Howell would arrange his affairs, Howell could arrange anything. Unfortunately he was in difficulties himself, having just been turned out of his house in Fulham. But difficulties were nothing to Howell. He had lived on the edge of disaster all his life.

Whistler's business became entangled with his own. He met a bill given to Whistler's builder "with the money out of my railway verdict now about to be paid." He pawned Whistler's pictures, on commission, or advanced a few pounds himself on a nocturne and a sealskin coat. He persuaded Messrs. Graves, the fine-art publishers, to issue engravings of Whistler's pictures and induced Graves to buy the "Carlyle," the "Mother," "Henry Irving," the portrait of "Maud," and two nocturnes. The "Carlyle" was reproduced in mezzotint and was very successful. Howell saw that Graves's confidence in Whistler had been restored and he proposed that the publisher should give Whistler one thousand pounds for a portrait of Disraeli and the right to engrave it. Graves agreed, and Howell hurried to Whistler with the joyful news.

The history of this transaction is extremely obscure. Whistler in later life used to tell vivid stories of his meeting with Disraeli—"Everything was most wonderful. We were the two artists together, recognizing each other at a glance" —but he admitted to his intimates that the whole tale was a fabrication, told for the pleasure of imitating Disraeli's voice. Howell's part is rather mysterious. Certainly he received some money from Graves, and Whistler received some money (but considerably less) from him. But Disraeli sat to Millais, and the Whistler project came to nothing.

Howell seems to have been incapable of a straightforward action. He had done Whistler a real service by inducing Graves to have prints made of his pictures, but he could not resist the temptation to cheat Whistler out of some of the proofs. When Whistler demanded his share he was told that none could be handed to him without Howell's consent. Whistler, in a rage, rushed off to Howell and demanded an explanation. Howell was full of apologies. Of course Whistler was entitled to as many of his own proofs as he desired; Howell would write a letter. He did so and read it aloud: "Give Mr. Whistler the proofs he desires. Yours very truly, C. A. H."

Whistler posted the letter himself and next day called at Graves' to collect his proofs. None was forthcoming. The assistant produced Howell's letter. Whistler flicked it out of his hand and read: "Of course you will not give Mr. Whistler the proofs he desires." Howell was playing for a few days' grace in which he could remove the prints himself, but the artist, now beside himself, sought out his slippery friend afresh and, flourishing his cane in Howell's face, demanded immediate satisfaction. Even then Howell had an answer ready.

"Of course I can explain it," he said. "Graves, stupid people, wrote to ask me if they were to put numbers on the proofs, large, big, horrid numbers, and I, having to

write to them for you, said: 'Of course you will not. Give
Mr. Whistler the proofs he desires.' Two separate sentences,
my dear man. I am so sorry. A million apologies." [1]

Whistler, mollified if not convinced, insisted that Howell should go with him to Graves to collect his proofs. Even
then he did not get them all, for some had been *mislaid* by
Howell and no one (but Howell) knew what had become
of them.

The story is worth telling, if only as an example of
the extraordinary difficulties in which Whistler found himself. He had quarreled with so many of his friends that
Howell was almost the only one left. He could help for the
moment, but in the end his activities left Whistler worse
off than ever.

The White House, planned in the days of his prosperity, had never been completely finished. Now it never
would be, at least by him. Nothing had gone right since he
quarreled with Leyland over the Peacock Room. *Then* he
had kept the ship-owner out of his own house. Now Leyland, who had bought up his debts, was his principal cred-
itor and was about to turn him out of his.

Whistler had probably never been entirely out of
debt since he came to London, perhaps since he sailed from
America. He was extremely careless in his housekeeping,
and when the failure of his libel action became known to

[1] For further stories of Howell see "Murray Marks and His Friends,"
by Dr. G. C. Williamson (London, 1919).

the tradesmen of Chelsea, they hurriedly presented their bills, some very large.

His reaction to his misfortunes was characteristic. Never had his *panache* floated more proudly, never had his walk been jauntier, his eye-glass more provocative. Bailiffs took up their quarters in his house, and he made them wait at table while he squandered his last shillings on dinner parties. Bills announcing the sale were pasted on his doorposts. They were loose and flapped in the wind. He insisted that they should be pasted on properly.

Such a condition of affairs could not continue, and in May, 1879, he was declared bankrupt. The difference between his assets and his liabilities was nearly three thousand pounds, and he had to face the loss of his house, his Blue China, and as many of his own pictures as remained in his possession. A committee, composed of Leyland, Howell, and Thomas Way, was appointed to administer his affairs, a bitter pill for Whistler, since, although friendly with Way and Howell, he regarded Leyland, somewhat unjustly, as responsible for his misfortunes. When the committee visited the White House to make inventory they found the studio empty except for three venomous caricatures of Leyland, one entitled "The Gold Scab-Eruption in Frilthy Lucre," representing the shipowner as a monstrous creature, half reptile, half bird, and covered with a hideous rash of sovereigns. The figure was seated at a piano, and the stool was a representation of the

White House. "Frilthy" instead of filthy is an allusion to Leyland's frilled shirt front.

The other enemy was Ruskin, and he too was not to escape unscathed. Among all his other occupations Whistler had found time to compose a pamphlet demonstrating once for all the utter uselessness of all critics.

It was Whistler's misfortune to be lured, in spite of himself, into criticism. Like Cyrano, whom he so much resembled in temperament, he was a master of fence. No one knew better than he how to land a swift thrust into his enemy's vitals. But his excursions into esthetics were a mistake, and even the famous "Ten o'Clock," packed as it is with good things, is full of quite indefensible propositions. Only the artist, he declared in his pamphlet of "Art and Art Critics," was capable of writing sound criticism, to which the proper reply would seem to be that the great artist does not waste his time doing anything of the kind. In reality, Whistler, with his craving for notoriety, was not quite honest in his attitude to criticism. What he objected to was unfavorable criticism. He was like the star actress who professes, in her dressing-room, the most complete contempt for the whole scribbling tribe, and early next morning sends out her maid to bring in every paper she can lay her hands on. Whistler even indulged in the terrible practice of carrying press cuttings in his pocket and compelling his friends to read them, and as such notices became toward the end of his life more and more favorable he carried more and more of them.

[ 198 ]

He was right in his contention that English art criticism, in the seventies at any rate, was vastly inferior to French, but the refusal to see any value in the critic's existence was merely his exasperation at an unfavorable verdict.

Certainly there is no room for the kind of criticism in which Ruskin indulged in "Fors Clavigera," but Whistler's subsequent fame was as much founded on criticism as the early misapprehension of his work against which he complained so bitterly. His readiness to join in the verbal battle delayed rather than hastened his final recognition, and, after all, Whistler's own criticism of his contemporaries was as one-sided as Ruskin's. Because Albert Moore admired the same type of feminine beauty and was himself an agreeable companion, he vastly exaggerated his importance as a painter, and he had a complete contempt for the work of Cézanne, because it differed so widely from his own. There is nothing surprising in this. Indeed the painter damages himself by too wide a sympathy. He becomes an eclectic and forgets to cultivate his own particular talent. Whistler, fortunately for himself, was completely impervious to the doctrines of later impressionism, but that very fact made him hopelessly limited as a critic. Nevertheless he seized on Ruskin's weak point at the end of his pamphlet when he cried, "Let him resign his present professorship, to fill the chair of ethics at the university," for an attempt to drag morals into painting was Ruskin's own peculiar limitation.

[ 199 ]

Meanwhile Whistler had found a friend, more trustworthy than Howell, who was to show him a way out of his difficulties. This was Ernest Brown, called affectionately "little Brown" by all who knew him. He called to see Whistler with regard to the "Billingsgate" etching which had been sold to the Portfolio. Whistler liked him and showed him over the house, remarking sadly that he was soon to lose it. Shortly afterwards Brown entered the employment of the Fine Art Society, and transformed it from the champion of Ruskin—the society had held the bank for the public subscription to pay his costs in the libel action—into Whistler's best friend. Brown induced his firm to buy several of Whistler's "London" plates, and then proposed that he should be sent out to Venice, with his expenses paid in advance, and with a free hand to produce a series of etchings.

This was just what Whistler wanted. He had no desire to remain in London for the humiliation of the sale. The scheme gave him some money to live on, and the work would distract his thoughts. He gladly accepted. Early in September, 1879, on the Sunday before his departure, he was alone with Howell in the White House. Whistler arranged with him for the disposal of a certain Japanese cabinet, to which Howell consented, fully intending to sell it for his own profit as soon as Whistler's back was turned. Then the weary artist climbed up a ladder and wrote over the lintel of his door: "Except the Lord build the house, they labor in vain that build it. E. W. Godwin, F. S. A., built this one." It was a flash of his ancestral Puritanism, only half laughing at itself. In the fall of 1879, the White House was sold to Harry Quilter, the art critic. But Whistler was already in Venice.

Venice, even at the end of the seventies, was not quite so tourist-ridden as it has since become. The Lido was already used by the Italians for sea-bathing, and once a year it was their custom to go there in gondolas, late at night, with guitars and mandolins, in order to watch the sunrise, but it was not yet a cosmopolitan resort.

Visitors to Venice were neither the very rich nor the poor tourists, but cultivated people, with some interest in music and literature and some knowledge of Italian art. The Brownings were still in residence, the ecclesiastical figure of Liszt could be seen in the piazza, George Eliot was there with her husband, and Ouida with her highly colored dreams. There Meissonnier exercised his eye for the minutiæ of surface texture, and the young Sargent his talent for summary statement.

It was a curious irony that brought the ruined Whistler to a city which his enemy Ruskin had made so peculiarly his own, but probably Whistler did not realize the fact. It is extremely unlikely that his reading embraced "The Stones of Venice." That was all to the good. To a man (or at least a painter) soaked in literature, Venice could be a dangerous place, and never more so than at that epoch.

[ 201 ]

Other painters had been there before him, and a man who cared for the past could hardly have avoided seeing Venice through Turner's eyes—the Grand Canal a line of shadowy golden palaces, the water between them gilded with the rays of a flamboyant sun. Fortunately Whistler was proof against the seduction of commonplace romanticism, and so he was not tempted to evoke the Venice of former epochs, to strive for the color of the sixteenth century, for the elegant frivolity of the eighteenth. Nor did he concentrate on sunsets. Grandiloquence of any kind was never a fault of his. He was too subtle, too feminine for that, and so he did not, immediately on his arrival, sit down in front of San Marco, or moor a gondola with his easel in it in front of the Bridge of Sighs. Instead he waited a long time before he set to work at all, wandering about the city through disused canals and unfrequented alleys, and so discovered, perhaps better than any artist before him, the modern Venice instead of the half-imagined image of its past. Venice gave herself to him with an intimacy that was the reward of his patient wooing, and so his vision of the city and its inhabitants is both authentic and curiously his own. To him it was a gray city, full of half-tones and subtle shadows, and the main object for which he had come —to make etchings—must have made him more eager to seek form than color. Perhaps the time when he arrived had something to do with this. First impressions of foreign cities are the most vivid, and can never afterwards be wholly obliterated. Whistler reached Venice in the middle of a gray November. It was as cold and bleak as only an Italian town can be in a month when few visitors are present to experience its wintry mood. This was to be the cause of some misunderstanding when his impressions of Venice were finally exhibited in London.

It was a long time before he settled down to work at all. He wanted first to absorb the atmosphere of the place, and, like a good American, one of his first actions was to call upon the American minister. That gentleman, Mr. Grist, with the friendly alacrity which seems to be the prerogative of American officials abroad, did all he could to make Whistler welcome, and accompanied his visitor about the city, pointing out the objects of interest.

Soon after the artist's arrival, the two men were strolling together in the neighborhood of the Bridge of Arts when Grist saw a group of young men emerging from the Accademia delle Belle Arte. He recognized them at once as "Duveneck's boys," the American art students who had studied under Frank Duveneck in Germany, and who had followed their master, first to Florence and then to Venice.

The minister accosted them and introduced his companion. Whistler was charmed, and said so in these words: "Whistler is charmed." The events of the last few years, the trial and the bankruptcy had caused Whistler to dramatize his own personality, and henceforth he always referred to himself in the third person. However odd "the

[ 203 ]

boys" may have thought it, they too were charmed to meet an artist of whom they had already heard so much.

Whistler himself had a particular reason for being pleased with this meeting. There is no doubt that he missed in Venice the public interest which surrounded his walks in London. He had grown accustomed also to the presence of admirers, and none of them had come with him on his travels. He saw at once that here was a new body-guard, a fresh group of enthusiastic young men, an audience for the comedy "Whistler," the perpetual performance of which had become one of the necessities of his existence. One of the group, Bacher, had been singled out by Grist for especial notice as "the boy who etches," and with him Whistler soon struck up a warm friendship.

Whistler was very poor, and his clothes were beginning to look seedy. He worked as he had never worked before, sitting for hours in the cold with a copperplate clasped in his frozen fingers. He lived in a succession of simple lodgings, and in one of these Maud joined him.

He took his meals in a cheap little eating-place, but even that was too expensive, and he cooked dishes for himself over a spirit lamp in his small sitting-room at San Barnaba. He taught his landlady to make polenta à l'américaine, and to fry fish to his taste, and soon the Sunday breakfasts began again. He had promised his mother never to paint or draw on Sundays, and so was at leisure to entertain his friends.

One of these friends discovered an old, dark printing office in the neighborhood of San Lorenzo, and it was here that the Venice plates were proved. Another—one of the "boys"—suggested that he should move to the house where most of them lived, the Casa Jankowitz, on the Riva, near the public gardens. He did so, contenting himself with a single room with windows looking toward the Doges' Palace, to San Giorgio and the Salute.

In his view the enemy, the cause of his financial embarrassments, had been not so much Ruskin as Leyland, and one of the two ornaments in his bare room was a photograph of the caricature of Leyland in the Peacock Room, Leyland as the grasping bird, with his claw on a pile of guineas. There was one other picture in his apartment, a photograph of himself with a sneer which Bacher found unpleasant. One evening he found a scorpion in his room, transfixed it with a pin and watched its vain efforts to strike him with its sting. He saw in the creature an image of himself, and he added to his butterfly signature a barbed and threatening tail. It was evident that Whistler had not come to Venice to forget.

His dress was, for him, comparatively inconspicuous. He wore a sack coat and, on fine days, white duck trousers. His white shirt had a very low turned-down collar, and instead of a tie he wore a long narrow black ribbon. Bacher has left a vivid picture of the way this ribbon flapped about in the wind, now streaming straight out in front, now

fluttering against the eye-glass, as if to emphasize the ges-
ticulations of its wearer. With evening dress he wore no
tie at all, and when this was noticed he remarked proudly
that "only Whistler would do it." On his head he had a
soft brown felt hat, pushed well back in order that the
white lock in his hair might not be hidden.

From Bacher's discreet narrative[2] it would be impossible to deduce the existence of Maud. It was not possible
to take her everywhere, but Maud had grown used to that
in London, and she was glad that Whistler had influential friends, whether they were willing to receive her or
not. In the evening, when the spring came, they would
sit with the rest of the world on the little café seats at the
Quadri or Florian's or the Orientale, and sip their coffee
and listen to the band.

Whistler realized that he had to make the most of his
time in Venice. He was not unhappy there, but (much as
he pretended to despise it) London was his platform, and
he longed to get back to it. Only he must not return empty-
handed. His return must be effective, silencing criticism
and winning new patrons.

He rose early and set out with his handsome gondolier,
Cavaldora, who rowed him about the canals or carried his
materials for him when he chose to walk. He was not much
interested, for the moment, in oil-painting, but he carried
a quantity of brown paper and two boxes of pastel colors,

[2] "With Whistler in Venice," by Otto Bacher (1908).

and (wherever he went) a supply of grounded plates for etching, carefully laid between the leaves of a book for fear they should be scratched.

He had come to Venice to etch, and the etchings remain the most important product of his stay, important not only for the influence they were to exert on the future of etching, but for the change they indicated in his own methods of going to work. Just as he had simplified his painting, so now he set about the simplification of his work on the copper. An interest in luminous shadow replaced his earlier interest in form, and instead of etching the roofs of Venice tile by tile, as he had etched the warehouses of the lower Thames twenty years before, he lavished all his skill on dark doorways through which hardly anything could be seen, corners of unimportant canals barely indicated with a scratch of the needle, suggestions of shimmering light on water, and phantom outlines of churches and palaces seen in the dim light across the lagoons.

There will always be controversy over these etchings of Whistler's. Those who like them will think of them as the fine flower of his genius, when, no longer tied by details of form, he could make one irregular line on the copper suggest both atmosphere and color. Those who prefer his earlier works will say that in his Venice plates Whistler degenerated into a vignettist and tempted weaker men to do the same. Certainly modern etching has repudiated Whistler's later manner and founded itself upon more

[ 207 ]

exacting masters, but when the reaction against looseness of handling has spent its force etchers may find a new inspiration in "The Riva," "The Doorway," and "Little Venice."

# CHAPTER VIII

### THE GROWTH OF THE LEGEND

WHISTLER was back in London in the autumn of 1880. In a world of November fog he set about printing his etchings of Venice. The sale of the White House had left him without a home, and a good deal of the work at the press was done in a studio in Air Street, a street much shortened since and completely transformed by the rebuilding of the Regent Quadrant. There was a market for his etchings, though at what seem now pathetically low prices. Etching was beginning to be fashionable, largely owing to the work of Seymour Haden, and although the two were enemies, Whistler could not be excluded from the public interest which had been evoked.

It was while he was printing in Air Street that he grew conscious of a curious change in his position. The admiration of "the boys" in Venice must have prepared him for it, but he always thought of himself as younger than he was, and he had not yet begun to look upon himself as "the Master." He was soon to acquire a "follower," for while he was at work at the press Mortimer Menpes arrived, and immediately became an ardent disciple. He offered Whis-

tler a room in his own house, fitted up with the necessary apparatus, and most of the Venetian etchings were
printed there. Whistler must have been very glad of these
marks of appreciation, for he found most of the world
against him, and the critics ready to pass his work off as
a joke.

But the ridicule with which the etchings were received
was nothing to that which awaited the exhibition of pastels.
Whistler had a genius for turning everything into a social
function, and his private view was no exception. The public was puzzled by an unfamiliar medium—chalk on brown
paper was not what they expected of an artist—and the
prices seemed excessive. Whistler took a perverse pleasure
in the confusion of visitors by assuring them that some of
the pastels took him at least half an hour. Punch made a
joke (not a very good joke) of the whole affair in an article
entitled: "Whistler's Wenice; or Pastels by Pastlethwaite."
The writer seemed to think that there was something a
little ill-bred in Whistler's daring to depart from the accepted conventions of easel-painting. The artist is represented as saying:

> "Well, Sir, I'm Master Jimmie Whistler, I am, and
> if I can do this sort o' thing with a shilling box o'
> paints from the Lowther Arcade, a few sheets of blot-
> ting paper, and some brown paper covers off the family
> jam-pots, I could do bigger work with improved
> materials, you bet."

Godwin, who had some power as a critic, as well as a reputation as an architect, was almost his only champion. He praised the pastels themselves and, what pleased Whistler even more, he wrote an article in the British Architect praising the decoration of the gallery. This, as always, Whistler had devised himself—a harmony of yellow-gold skirting, dull yellow-green cloth walls, a molding of green-gold, and a frieze and ceiling of pale reddish brown. The frames were either of yellow-gold or of green-gold, cunningly mixed, and as a background for the brown-paper pastels the scheme could hardly be bettered.

Most of the critics were hostile, but they could not spoil the market for the pastels. Four hundred pounds' worth was sold the first day, and the sum had risen to a thousand pounds before the exhibition closed. It was enough to save Whistler from immediate anxiety, but not enough to guarantee his future. Ruskin's blow at his credit as a painter had left its mark on the public memory, and his oil pictures were still unsalable, in spite of the success of his smaller work. What was even more serious, no new sitters came to be painted. Yet Whistler set about rebuilding his existence as much as possible on the old plan.

His mother died in 1881, but as she had been an invalid at Hastings for the five years previous, it did not affect his domestic arrangements. Maud was still with him, and Whistler, full of hope for the fashionable crowd that was to throng his doors, took a new studio at No. 13 Tite Street, near enough to the White House to sharpen his anger against those who had deprived him of it.

Harry Quilter presented a double target for the artist's resentment, for not only had he succeeded Whistler as occupant of the White House but he had succeeded Whistler's old enemy, Tom Taylor, as art critic of the Times. He was a somewhat careless writer, and Whistler took great delight in pouncing on his slips. The worst was when he described a water-color of Ruskin by Herkomer as "the first oil portrait we have ever seen of our great art critic!" Whistler suggested, in a letter to the World, that if Quilter suffered from such chronic catarrh that he could not *smell* the difference between oil and water-color, he ought at least "to inquire." Later Quilter mistook a photogravure reproduction of a pen-and-ink drawing for an etching, and Whistler reminded him of his previous mistake in one of his best letters.

No, he never would ask—he liked his pot-shots at things; it used to give a sort of sporting interest to his speculations about pictures. And so he was ever obstinate—or anyone at the Fine Art Society would have told him the difference between an etching and a photograph.

Whistler's wit was sharpened in the early eighties by the sudden appearance of a rival, for a rival he was, although Whistler chose at first to regard him as a disciple only. He had, apparently, good reason to do so.

[ 212 ]

Oscar Wilde went up to Magdalen College, Oxford, in 1875, and before he went down four years later had acquired a reputation far beyond the limits of the university. He wore his hair long (like Whistler), he collected Blue China (Whistler had been collecting it since the early sixties), and he decorated his rooms with peacock feathers (in 1878 Whistler was painting the Peacock Room). Wilde embodied in his own person all the esthetic influences for which Whistler himself was directly responsible.

Whistler returned from Venice to find Wilde the accepted hero of a new movement, the apostle of a new cult. Since Whistler regarded himself as the deity of this new religion, he had no objection to the evangelist, at least for a time. But Wilde with all his limitations was something very much more than the disciple of Whistler, and the trouble which arose between the two men had its source in the fact that while Wilde regarded Whistler as his equal, Whistler, who tolerated no equals, regarded Wilde as a hanger-on.

In the public mind they were at first confused, and when "Patience" was put on the stage in 1881, Bunthorne, the "esthetic" hero, was a mixture of both. Punch tried to set the matter right by an imaginary conversation between Whistler and Wilde, in which the poet and the painter discussed art and life together. Wilde was in the provinces and wired to Whistler:

[ 213 ]

Punch too ridiculous—when you and I are together we never talk about anything except ourselves.

Whistler received the telegram with mixed feelings.
So the young man was assuming equality! He wired back:

No, no, Oscar, you forget—when you and I are
together, we never talk about anything except me.

There was never any question between Wilde and
Whistler of the kind of friendship that had existed between
Whistler and Fantin or between Whistler and Moore. They
went about together, they bandied witticisms over the
dinner tables of their friends, but although their real fame
was different, the kind of notoriety on which they both
relied was too similar not to provoke rivalry and, ultimately, hostility.

Wilde as a literary man had a weapon which Whistler could use only occasionally, and his criticisms of Whistler's work in the public press were not of the ecstatic pros-
trate kind which the artist expected. Even his praise had a
tang of raillery: "For that he is one of the greatest artists
of the world is my opinion, and I may add that in this opinion, Mr. Whistler himself entirely concurs!"

To Whistler, Wilde's pretensions as the Apostle of
Estheticism were merely ridiculous, and when Wilde was
invited to lecture in America—that same America which
still ignored Whistler as completely as if he had never been
born—Whistler was secretly outraged. Punch made merry

[ 214 ]

over the proposed trip with a parodied version of Ossian: "The Son of Cultcha has gone to the Land of Strangers"; and Whistler told him that, with the exception of his epigrams, he talked "like Sidney Colvin [1] in the provinces," and that, with the exception of his knee-breeches, he dressed like 'Arry Quilter.

He would never admit that Wilde knew anything about art at all, and he published his contempt to the world.

"What has Oscar in common with Art? except that he dines at our tables and picks from our platters the plums for the pudding he peddles in the provinces. Oscar—the amiable, irresponsible, esurient Oscar—with no more sense of a picture than of the fit of a coat, has the courage of the opinions . . . of others."

Wilde was nettled, and suggested that "with our James vulgarity begins at home." To which Whistler replied: "'A poor thing,' Oscar! but, for once, I suppose your own."

The "amiable Oscar"! Whistler, with his usual acumen, had picked on Wilde's principal charm as a man and his principal weakness in a controversy of this kind. For Wilde *was* amiable while Whistler was not, and they were fighting with unequal weapons. Wilde's wit, at its best, is not personal at all ("a cynic is a man who knows the price of everything and the value of nothing") while Whistler's

[1] Then Slade Professor.

[ 215 ]

was nothing else. Yet it did not go very deep, for it is only from profound natures that the really annihilating remark can come. A remark like that of Degas on Meissonnier's "Les Cuirassiers" ("It's all iron except the cuirasses!") was forever beyond him. He aimed a pea-shooter, not a machine-gun. His sarcasm, although painful, was more high-spirited than malicious, and he would frequently invent witticisms and then look round for someone to attach them to. The true ironist does not work in this way. He wants to destroy. Whistler loved a fight, but he really cared little whether he wounded his opponent or not so long as the audience admired his sword-play. A wit of Whistler's caliber makes a good many enemies, but even more friends; the coiner of really devastating phrases is apt to make an enemy of the whole human race. In Degas's company Whistler was silent, mindful perhaps of the master's verdict on himself. "You behave," said Degas, "as if you had no talent." But really savage sarcasm is very rare in England, and Whistler's was sharp enough for most of his contemporaries.

Whistler was feared and disliked by the academicians and by the older men generally, but there was a growing body of younger artists who were beginning to look upon him as master. It was not so much, perhaps, that they copied either his subject matter or his technique, but they were conscious that he represented a larger tradition of painting than the one current in England; and his very

[ 216 ]

pugnacity and eccentricity were a protest in which they willingly joined against the smugness of official art. He was, too, neglected and underestimated; and with the generosity of youth they flocked round him as Whistler and his friends had flocked round Courbet.

Menpes has already been mentioned, but Walter Richard Sickert was a more important "follower," for it was he who was to carry on something of the Whistler tradition in later years. Others were Sidney Starr, Harper Pennington (one of Duveneck's boys) and Anthony Ludovici and William Stott. The "followers" were not exactly pupils, for Whistler was too selfish to trouble himself about them. "You must be occupied with the master," he said, "not with yourselves. There is plenty to be done." They ran his errands, they helped to print his plates, but (more important from Whistler's point of view) they formed a bodyguard when he walked abroad. In restaurants and in the streets they made him the center of a noisy crowd. They advertised him everywhere. They were terribly bad for him, and terribly necessary.

Whistler had no resources on which he could fall back when he was alone. He read nothing either in French or English, although from their frequent occurrence in his conversation he seems once to have read Bret Harte and Edgar Allan Poe. Music meant nothing to him whatever, although he liked to use musical terms. Perhaps the fondness for applying such terms to other arts is the surest sign of the unmusical mind. He took no interest in any painting but his own, and never hung upon his walls any work that he had not painted himself. He was fond of the theater, but that was part of his love of a crowd. His dread of solitude was almost pathological. With no one to "take notice" he was miserable and ill at ease, and this craving to be looked at was at the bottom of his eccentricity and of his unacknowledged love of London. In the country there was no one to remark the pink bows on his dancing pumps or the long white cane, and in Paris such things have no prestige. But London, London of the eighties, was the perfect background. Bond Street the ideal stage.

In his early days in Paris he had been noticeable for his large straw hat perched jauntily on the top of his abundant curls. When he first came to London he tried to introduce the very sensible fashion of wearing white duck in the summer. He returned from Venice in a cloak so extraordinary that his more formal English friends were ashamed to be seen in the street with him, but he soon discarded it for what became his typical costume. This consisted of a well-cut black frock coat, worn rather long, a very tall silk hat with flat brim (an idea he had borrowed from the painter Chase), white trousers, and patent leather pumps, occasionally worn with colored bows. In his right hand he carried a long cane almost as tall as himself, and in his eye twinkled the famous monocle, with which to stare the bourgeois out of countenance.

In such a get-up there was less of dandyism than of the desire for advertisement. The true dandy places himself just this side of the line that divides elegance from eccentricity. He concentrates on cut rather than color, and however much attention he may give to the minor details of his costume would never insult the English eye with pink bows on patent-leather shoes. For the very word dandy is English, and dandyism a peculiarly English thing. It must not stray too far from current fashion on penalty of parting from "good form," a superstition for which Whistler, fortunately for his own notoriety, cared nothing. Mortimer Menpes assures us that "the idea of wearing white duck trousers with a black coat was conceived, not in order to be unlike other people, but because they formed a harmony in black and white which he loved." Sometimes he relieved the black and white with a touch of delicate color. Val Prinsep, the painter, met Whistler going to a dinner party. "With his overcoat thrown back he showed a great expanse of shirt front, and in his waistcoat was stuck a salmon-colored silk handkerchief." In his hand he carried a long slender wand.

At the present day such a colored handkerchief would make a man look like a waiter or a low comedian, but Prinsep was not astounded at the color of the handkerchief; he was only afraid that Whistler would lose it. He said so, and thrust the square of colored silk out of sight.

[ 219 ]

"Good God!" cried Whistler, "what are you doing? You've destroyed my precious note of color." Hastily, he rearranged the delicately tinted folds and passed on his way, flourishing the long white wand.

In spite of such eccentricities, Whistler had excellent taste, and if he did not respect the English convention sufficiently to conform to it, he never stumbled, as Wilde did, into fancy dress. His amusing reproof to Wilde shows how different were their attitudes. Wilde had been seen getting out of a cab dressed in a long green frogged overcoat à la polonaise, and Whistler wrote to him to "restore those things to Nathan's, and never again let me find you masquerading the streets of my Chelsea in the combined costumes of Kossuth and Mr. Mantalini."

In this Whistler was not only protesting in the name of good taste, he was obeying a sound psychological instinct. If the artist seeks to gain attention by some eccentricity of attire it should always be the same eccentricity, or the public gets confused. The principle is well understood in modern commercial advertising, with its frequent use of some symbolic personage who is always dressed in the same way. The mere focusing of attention is not enough, and Whistler took care that the inevitable question: "Who is that?" should always be followed by an answer as inevitable: "That is Whistler."

It is a difficult question how far an artist is justified in using methods of publicity. Certainly to live quietly and remote from one's fellows is not the way to enjoy fame before one's death. True fame burgeons slowly while notoriety is a weed that grows with the rapidity of the beanstalk. It is sometimes possible to use it as a prop for the tender plant of true fame, and in this Whistler, more than anyone else, was to succeed.

In an artist, the desire to be talked about may not spring altogether from personal vanity. Fame, even if artificial, is not only a balm, it is a tonic, and some kind of recognition is essential if that artist is to go on working at all. If he is a poor man it is the only alternative to starvation; if he is well provided for in material things it is none the less necessary for his well-being. Without it his talent is dwarfed and stunted, as we can hardly doubt that Blake's talent was dwarfed and stunted by too narrow a circle of admirers. Even poetry, most self-contained of all the arts, suffers by lack of an audience, and other artists are not so fortunate as the poet. The unacknowledged architect or actor is deprived even of the materials of his craft. Sculptors are perpetually hampered by the lack of stuff to work in, and painters only less so. But even given the materials, for lack of a commission the artist may never even suspect his own power. The existence of the vast ceiling of the Sistine Chapel was an essential part of Michelangelo's inspiration. An artist must have some kind of fame during his lifetime if he is to do his best work.

If that is so, then the artist is justified in organizing his own fame if he can, or in other words, publicity is an essential part of his business.

[ 221 ]

Having produced his work of art the artist must see to it that it is not left on his hands. The presence of rows of canvases not only decreases the size of a painter's studio; it cramps his inspiration. He must let people know there is work to be bought and he must induce them to buy it.

But personal notoriety is a very dangerous thing. It antagonizes as many as it attracts, and very often a serious artist (as Whistler was) suffers from the reputation for flippancy which he has himself labored to build up. The craving for public notice is, however, largely a matter of temperament. Some great artists have loved posturing and some have not, and it is only the posturing mediocre artist who is unforgivable. The best excuse for Whistler's behavior, whether calculated or not to increase his immediate fame, is that he could not help it.

He was, no doubt, fortunate in his epoch. Advertising was in its infancy, and he had all the advantages of the pioneer. Then, too, people still strolled, and, not being in perpetual danger from the surrounding traffic, could pause to stare. Fame, like everything else, has been canned, and the world no longer enjoys its notables in the flesh but in the illustrated papers. If Whistler had lived today, he would have been compelled to have himself photographed upside down. In the eighties it was sufficient to stroll down Bond Street.

He would take a cab from Chelsea, and alight in the famous thoroughfare, preferably with a "follower," in order to insure at least one attentive member of the audience. He would walk into any exhibitions that were open, adjust his eye-glass, give his harsh mocking laugh, and walk out into the street again. Small wonder that he found himself unpopular. He would visit his tailor, and by the aid of that mixture of effrontery and charm which was his most powerful weapon, he would soon concentrate the attention of the entire establishment upon himself. Customers too would be drawn into the circle, until only one question in the world existed for anybody present: Did Whistler's coat fit? That urgent matter settled, Whistler would gather up his skirts (the phrase is Mortimer Menpes's and throws a vivid light on the whole affair) and step daintily into the street. At the barber's the same game! Everyone else's hair would be neglected while Whistler's plentiful mop was attended to, and when it had been cut its wilful disarray had to be carefully arranged anew with due regard to the position of the famous white lock.

In the street he would pause before shop windows, gesticulating and uttering shrill cries on the rare occasions when he saw something he liked, giving his famous "Ha! ha!" when he saw something typical of the "Islanders'" stupidity. In London such a man could hardly fail to be the center of a constant if shifting crowd. His every walk abroad spread his legend farther.

Even in the studio he preferred not to be alone, and

[ 223 ]

unlike most artists seems to have been glad of company even when he was working. Uncongenial visitors he knew well how to chase away, and he took a perverse pleasure in assuming the mountebank to those whom he considered stupid. He displayed his work to the accompaniment of incessant patter. His long thin hands were never still for an instant—whisking out the drawings, adjusting his monocle, gesticulating in the air—while, as every work appeared, the mouth would form, only half interrogatively, the word "Pretty?"

His work at this period was always being interrupted by the claims of social life. His mantelpiece was littered with cards of invitation to dinners, soirées, and garden parties. Maud could not have seen very much of him, for her irregular position made it impossible to invite her everywhere, and Whistler frequently dined at one of his many clubs. He belonged to the Arts, the Hogarth, the Chelsea Arts, the Arundel, the Beefsteak, and the Beaufort Grill Club. He was once put up for the Savile, but someone objected, and he was never elected. There must have been many members of all his clubs who detested him, but in most he had a circle of admirers willing to fight his battles.

The American artist Alden Weir was once walking in Piccadilly when he met Whistler. The latter asked him to dine at his club and Weir consented. Whistler called a hansom and when they arrived at his first club got out, asking Weir to remain in the cab. He returned in a moment and explained to his guest that it was quite impossible to dine at *that* club because there was mutton on the menu. They drove to the next, where Whistler again alighted. He was back almost instantly saying that So-and-so was in the club and he didn't like his face. They drove on, a similar scene being enacted at every one of Whistler's clubs until the list was exhausted. The farceur, with many apologies, then suggested that Weir should dine with him in Chelsea. Weir, by this time very hungry, was glad to dine anywhere, but was astonished to find on arrival at Whistler's house that a large party of guests had been awaiting their astounding host for two hours or more. Weir was the only one not in evening dress, except Whistler, who kept everybody waiting a little longer while he changed.

He was always late, by habit and on principle, and he hated to go to bed before the small hours of the morning. After a theater he always went to the Hogarth Club, where he was immediately surrounded by a group of admirers, some sitting on the floor at his feet and gazing up at him with rapture. Whistler sat enthroned, a tiny glass of liqueur in one hand, the other playing with his eye-glass or making passes in the air, his shrill voice and loud laugh echoing through the club. When he was tired of it he would persuade some of the young men to walk home with him to Chelsea, if the night was fine.

To be with him on these occasions was to see Whistler at his best. As the river was reached, with its long low banks, its distant lights, the mysterious shapes of boats and barges half seen through the darkness, a change would come over him. The man-about-town would fall away, and the artist reassert himself. The beauty of the Thames at midnight melted the hard shell of his egotism. He forgot to advertise and began to create, or at least to observe and feel. The method employed was that which had been taught to his friends in Paris by Lecoq de Boisbaudran, and which Whistler had learned from them. He imparted it to his followers, and made them listen while he recited the scene he had just observed. He would look for a long time at some particular group of objects, and then, turning his back, would describe them, noting particularly the gradation of color and the relation of tone.

"Look," he would say, "at that golden interior with the two spots of light, and that old woman with the checkered shawl. See the warm purple tone outside going up to the green of the sky, and the shadows from the windows thrown on the ground. What an exquisite lacework they form." Next morning Menpes would find him at work on a nocturne.

He loved the night, or rather the twilight, as ardently as the late impressionists used to love the sunshine, but his method was the very reverse of theirs. He never strove to convert himself into the lens of a camera, recording as accurately as possible any aspect of nature that was placed before him. He composed everything (it was the very essence of his method) before he put it into his picture. He wanted a harmony, not a transcript, and those paintings or pastels which were done out of doors he logically entitled "Notes." As long ago as the early sixties he had written to Fantin: "Painting after nature is something one should do at home."

For his etchings he adopted the opposite method, drawing them on the copper direct from nature, and never troubling to reverse. Most modern etchers, making a plate of St. James's Palace, would make a preliminary drawing of an elaborate kind, reverse it, and transfer it to the plate. Whistler cared very little for exact topography. What he was interested in, especially in his later plates, was atmosphere and .movement, and his plate of St. James's Street is so full of both that we do not trouble to reflect that the palace has slipped into the wrong corner or that the carriages are advancing on the wrong side of the street. He always carried a supply of grounded plates with him, or rather the followers carried them for him, ready for the master's use whenever the fancy seized him. If people wished to be devoted Whistler knew how to make use of them.

In the winter of 1883–4, Sickert and Menpes went with him to Cornwall, where they led a not altogether placid existence. Whistler, traveling, could be a mixture of spoilt

prima-donna and naughty child, and he does not seem to
have cared much for Cornwall when he got there. He insisted on wearing his square-toed patent-leather pumps
even for long walks, and the flinty roads around St. Ives
must have worn out not a few. He was irritated, too, by not
being able to win the confidence of the dour fisher-folk. To
them he was just a lunatic from London, while they made
friends with Sickert readily enough. Sickert had the unfair
advantage also of having been in those remote parts before
as an actor in a touring company. Now Whistler acted in
vain, he could not win them over. Packets arrived at their
lodging: "A parcel of fish for Mr. Sickert." Whistler was
furious, and took Sickert to task for his presumption. "It
is the master who should receive these gifts," he said.

However, his wounded vanity was soon to receive welcome balm, for while he was in Cornwall, a movement
was set on foot in London to make him a member of the
old and respectable Society of British Artists. Whistler, to
his friends' surprise, was not at all averse from the project.
He was no ferocious independent, despising all societies
of artists. On the contrary he liked them, and official
recognition, when he could get it, pleased him. No one
ever wore the ribbon of the Legion of Honor more
proudly than he was to do in his later years.

Accounts vary somewhat and it is not easy to say
which side made the first overtures. Jacomb-Hood, in his
reminiscences, says that it was William Ingram who hit on

the idea of getting Whistler elected. Whistler, no doubt, heard something of this, and with all his love of an intrigue he got Sickert to indicate to Anthony Ludovici his willingness to join. Ludovici, who had been a member since 1878 and was in close touch with the younger men, told the strange news to John Burr, the president, who was pleased. The other officials were less elated, the vice-president, Holyoake, being frankly incredulous. The honorary secretary, Roberts, was afraid that his colonel in the Artists' Rifles—no less a person than Leighton—would disapprove. A great many of the members were bitterly hostile, but they were disorganized and powerless against a determined faction. Whistler was elected to the society.

The ambitions of his supporters, however, went much further than his mere membership. Secret meetings were held in Jacomb-Hood's studio, and the newly discovered political weapon of the "caucus" was put into operation. The partizans of Whistler voted solidly for him on every occasion, and in the end, against the divided vote of the rest of the society, he was elected president.

Whistler was delighted. Not only was his election a proof of confidence on the part of the younger men, but it placed him, if only temporarily, in a strong strategic position from which he could sally forth at will to harry his enemies. Punch's prophecy that he would prove a veritable King Stork was entirely justified. He turned the society upside-down.

There was no more election of painters for the sake of their subscriptions, no more overcrowding of the walls with mediocre paintings, no more willingness to accept the scourings of the Royal Academy. The rooms were re-decorated, a velarium was introduced to temper the light, and the pictures were all spaced out according to Whistler-ian principles. To the horror of the sabbatarian members, the new president introduced Sunday tea-parties, with charming girls in frocks to match the decorations, handing round bread-and-butter. Society, ever on the alert for a new amusement, flocked to Suffolk Street to show off its new gowns and chat with Oscar Wilde and the president himself.

This kind of thing could not long continue. It was no consolation to the members whose work had been excluded that the exhibitions were such a social success. They natu-rally preferred more solid patrons who come not to admire Whistler, but to buy pictures, and the bigger the better. The committee meetings of the society were so many battlegrounds, Whistler in perpetual evening dress, his eye-glass shining, his white lock floating like an oriflamme, be-leaguered on the platform by a hostile crowd of indignant British artists. He kept them at bay for a surprisingly long time, and enjoyed himself thoroughly in the process.

The dissatisfied members had learned a lesson from their opponents, and they banded together to make sure that Whistler was not elected again. Their ranks were reenforced by those who, although they might have no objection to Whistler himself, yet feared his extravagance in redecorating the galleries and his avowed policy of putting merit above cash returns. Even his adroitness in preparing an address for the Queen's Jubilee, and the consequent transformation of the Society of British Artists into the Royal Society of British Artists, failed to reconcile the irreconcilables.

His chief opponent throughout his presidency was an artist named Wyke Bayliss, whom Whistler annoyed by always referring to as "Mr. Baillie." Whistler was constitutionally incapable of resisting even so obvious a pin-prick as that, but, as so often, he redeemed himself by a touch of his habitual grace. For Bayliss bethought himself in the end of calling Whistler "Mr. Whistle." *"Touché,"* cried Whistler, falling into the position of a fencer courteously acknowledging a hit. When Whistler fell, Wyke Bayliss was elected in his place and was shortly afterwards created a knight for his services to British art, if not to the British Artists. Twenty-five other members resigned with the outgoing president, and Whistler provided champagne to toast their departure. "The Artists have come out," he said, "and the British remain."

The subsequent squabble over the notice board need not detain us here. It was natural that Whistler should feel a little bitter. He really had done his best for the society, and had not, as some members feared at the time of his election, used it merely for his own glorification. He had made it recognized abroad as it has never been before or since, and he even induced two distinguished foreign artists—Alfred Stevens and Monet—to become honorary members. His failure was regrettable not only because of its effect on the society, but because of its effect upon himself. It intensified his feeling that he was always bound to be at war with stupidity, it increased his contempt for the British public, and it convinced him more than ever that he was right.

Meanwhile Whistler was far from prosperous, and the studio in Tite Street, whether for financial reasons or not, was abandoned. Maud never seems to have taken up her quarters there. After Venice she lived with Whistler in Alderney Street, but she went to Paris for the birth of her daughter, and on her return the lodgings were probably too small. They moved into the "Pink Palace," Fulham, and then into a kind of close off Fulham Road, now demolished. It was called the Vale, and was a favorite retreat for artists. Stirling Lee, the sculptor, lived there, William De Morgan made some of his pots there, and it gave its name to the Vale Press.

Whistler's house in the Vale was of the square type with iron verandas typical of the early nineteenth century in London. At the back it had a largish garden, left to run wild, for Whistler had little money to spare for improving his property. He had little enough for furnishing. For-

LA LECTURE: *By Fantin-Latour. In*
*the Musée de Lyon.*

PORTRAIT OF WHISTLER'S
MOTHER: *In the Musée du
Luxembourg.*

tunately, walls distempered yellow, Chinese matting on the floor, and the absence of all but the most necessary furniture, comprised his ideal scheme for decoration. He was free from the ostentation that demands luxurious surroundings, and there is every reason to believe he was very happy there.

His pamphlet against critics had given him a taste for writing, and since, in the absence of commissions for portraits, he had time on his hands, he set about expounding the principles of his art in a lecture.

Whistler never did anything carelessly. Everything, from his personal appearance to his portraits, from the decoration of his house to the butterfly buttonholes he gave away at a private view, was contrived with conscious artistry. There was none of the squandering of more robust genius. Not even a witticism was wasted. His failures were not things he had "thrown off," but things that had defeated him after desperate strivings, for his method had its own limitations.

When he turned to literature he brought to it the same meticulous care which distinguished every other department of his life. An amateur he was not, for he imparted a professional touch into everything he did. His written works, therefore, have none of the easy charm of some occasional writers. There is no self-revelation, but a hard metallic surface below which it is impossible to penetrate.

He gave immense labor to the polishing of his lecture.

[ 233 ]

It was to be his manifesto, and every word mattered. He was careful too that it should have its proper setting, just as he was anxious that his pictures should be suitably framed and appropriately hung. He chose the old St. James's Hall (now replaced by a hotel), partly on account of its excellent acoustics, and partly because, being situated in Piccadilly, it was conveniently near the houses of his fashionable friends. A prophet of Ruskin's make thought that a little hardship was good for an audience. If people wished to hear the gospel of art in conditions more comfortable than those in which they listened to the gospel of religion, they were probably unworthy of the Message and had better stay away. Whistler's method was the exact opposite. He decided to make his audience as comfortable as possible. They were not even to hurry over their dinners. Far better that the men should linger over their port and the women over their scandal, so that both might come to his lecture in a more exalted frame of mind. Whistler never deluded himself into the belief that art, for the majority of Englishmen, was anything but a luxury.

His lecture, therefore, was fixed for ten o'clock, and Piccadilly was choked with the elegant carriages whose late occupants moved leisurely to their places in St. James's Hall. Whistler appeared in beautifully cut evening dress, his white hands moving like a conjurer's, his eye-glass twinkling. He apologized to his audience for appearing before them in the character of the Preacher. He deplored the efforts of those (like Ruskin, although he did not men-

tion him) who had tried to popularize art. "Alas! ladies
and gentlemen, Art has been maligned. She has nought in
common with such practices. She is a goddess of dainty
thought—reticent of habit, abjuring all obtrusiveness, pur-
posing in no way to better others." The protest against
ethical irrelevance is well justified, but "dainty thought"
is a piece of special pleading.

Whistler went on to defend the complete absorption of
the artist in his own pursuits, and ridiculed the notion that
great masters had ever lived in common understanding
with their patrons. "There never was an artistic period.
There never was an art-loving nation," but he admitted that
there was a time when "the Amateur was unknown—
and the Dilettante undreamed of," and when people were
surrounded with beautiful things because there were no
other. If this Golden Age was not an artistic period it
is hard to see what could be implied by the term. Whistler declared that "the world was flooded with all that
was beautiful, until there arose a new class, who discovered the cheap, and foresaw fortune in the future of
the sham"; but he omitted to say how this astonishing
change came about, and whose fault it was, if the fault
were anyone's.

He was on surer ground in protesting against that
heresy of "truth to nature" which had vitiated so much of
Ruskin's criticism. "Nature contains the elements, in color
and form, of all pictures, as the keyboard contains the
notes of all music.

[ 235 ]

"But the artist is born to pick and choose, and group with science these elements that the result may be beautiful—as the musician gathers his notes and forms his chords, until he brings forth from chaos, glorious harmony.

"To say to the painter that Nature is to be taken as she is, is to say to the player that he may sit on the piano."

It must seem strange to us, after the opposite excesses of some modern painting, that there was ever anything astonishing, to a cultivated audience, in the mild and reasonable doctrine propounded by Whistler. But he, having disposed of one heresy, proceeded to fall headlong into another. For the "vice of subject" is no less a vice when the painter looks to the beauties of the objects before him, than when he searches out their moral significance, and it is simply not true that the brilliant sunshine which delights the holiday-maker, and lights up the windows of the Crystal Palace, causes the painter to turn aside and shut his eyes. He does if he is Whistler; he does not if he is Monet.

In the passage that followed, Whistler's voice grew warm and eloquent. "And when," he cried, "the evening mist clothes the riverside with poetry, as with a veil, and the poor buildings lose themselves in the dim sky, and the warehouses are palaces in the night, and the whole city hangs in the heavens, and fairyland is before us—then the wayfarer hastens home; the working man and the cultured one; the wise man and the one of pleasure cease to understand, as they have ceased to see, and Nature, who for once has sung in tune, sings her exquisite song to the artist alone, her son and her master—her son in that he loves her, her master in that he knows her."

The passage shows that Whistler could write; it is also an admirable summary of what he chose to paint, but as esthetic doctrine it is quite worthless. Romanticism does not change its nature because it puts forward the clock, and it requires only a few years of the filtering down of taste for some esthetic revolutionary to denounce a "very foolish" twilight as bitterly as Whistler had just denounced "a very foolish sunset."

Manet, when he wished to simplify, did so frankly. He did not pretend that the outlines were blurred in mist and the contours lost in shadow. But Manet and Whistler, although their art had a common source, had now flowed far apart, and with the later developments of impressionism, Whistler had no sympathy whatever.

Whistler went on, quite rightly, to protest against the literary bias of contemporary critics, and against the whole notion, then so common, that painting was made finer by depicting some noble incident or improving anecdote. Such a complaint is now largely obsolete, although the passage that followed in Whistler's lecture might still find its mark.

"There are those also, somber of mien, and wise with the wisdom of books, who frequent museums and burrow in crypts; collecting—comparing—compiling—classifying—contradicting.

[ 237 ]

"Experts these—for whom a date is an accomplishment —a hall-mark, success!

"Careful in scrutiny are they, and conscientious of judgment, establishing, with due weight, unimportant reputations, discovering the picture by the stain on the back —testing the torso by the leg that is missing . . . disputatious and dictatorial concerning the birthplace of inferior persons—speculating, in much writing, upon the great worth of bad work."

Whistler never wrote anything else at once so witty and so wise. Would that his words could be framed and exhibited in conspicuous places in all the principal auction rooms of Europe!

The lecturer was no more merciful to the appointed sages of the universities. Ruskin probably never read the "Ten o'Clock," but the audience must have known who was meant when Whistler spoke of the prophet "crying out, and cutting himself—while the gods hear not.

"Gentle priest of the Philistine . . . he ambles pleasantly from all point, and through many volumes, escaping scientific assertion—'babbles of green fields.' "

Whistler, with his aristocratic instincts, had a great contempt for the effort to educate the masses which engaged Ruskin's whole strength. The "one unspoken sympathy that pervades humanity is—Vulgarity!" But Whistler had no liking for the Esthetes either, and the fashionable ranks of his audience must have stirred with pleasure as he be-

ought them to listen to no dress-reformers, but to seek
elegance before all things. "Your own instinct," he told
them, "is near the truth—your own wit far surer guide
han the untaught ventures of thick-heeled Apollos." Art,
he told them, just happened, and nothing they could do
would help to bring it about. "We have then but to wait
until—with the mark of the gods upon him—there come
among us again the chosen—who shall continue what has
gone before. Satisfied that, even were he never to appear,
he story of the beautiful is already complete—hewn in
he marbles of the Parthenon—and broidered with the
birds, upon the fan of Hokusai—at the foot of Fujiyama."

No wonder the lecture was a success! No wonder the
ashionable ladies and gentlemen went home well pleased
with the lecturer and with themselves! Here was no grum-
bling prophet telling them that they must scrub floors and
dig roads before they had the right even to look at art.
Here was no obsession with social problems, but elegance
peaking to elegance and saying that all was well. The invitation cards stood thicker upon Whistler's mantelpiece
han they had ever stood before.

Meanwhile, Whistler's domestic arrangements were
once more breaking up. Maud was by no means the placid
companion that Jo had been. Both she and Whistler were
high-tempered, and they began to get on each other's
nerves. Her health had been ruined in Venice and, having
seen him through the worst years of his bankruptcy and

subsequent poverty, she was naturally a little resentful of some of his new friends. Whistler had nothing of the libertine in his composition, but he loved feminine society especially when it was elegant and sophisticated. Maud' elegance had been one of the reasons for the dismissal of Jo. Perhaps the difficult years had robbed her of something that once attracted Whistler. He began to take great pleasure in the company of Mrs. Godwin, whom he met while helping to superintend the entertainments given by Lady Archibald Campbell in the grounds of Coombe House.

Whistler found Mrs. Godwin particularly attractive Maud represented the English type; Mrs. Godwin is said to have been very French in appearance; handsome, and with "daredevil eyes." She was the daughter of John Birnie Philip, the sculptor, and accustomed to the ways of artists. Whistler appealed to her, and she spent much of her time with him.

Perhaps Whistler's reaction against the English type of woman was part of his revulsion against all things English. His thoughts were turning once more to France, and he was thinking of going to live there and abandoning London forever. Godwin hardly pretended to be faithful to his wife, his love affairs were notorious, and Mrs. Godwin must have found some consolation in the avowed affection of Whistler. An obstacle was removed from their path by her husband's death in 1886. His funeral, which took place in the country, was turned into a kind of picnic

Whistler, Mrs. Godwin, and Lady Archibald Campbell attended it, riding in a country wagon, and the second lady was quick to notice that her companions already seemed very fond of each other.

Mrs. Godwin lived in Chelsea, and became an habitué of Whistler's studio, often sitting there for hours, to the serious interruption of his work. Whistler was painting a picture of Lady Archibald, but even that friendly woman began to resent the constant presence of "the little widdie." Maud, naturally enough, resented it strongly. She saw that at last a serious rival had arisen, and that she would have to fight to keep Whistler's affection. Unfortunately, she was not a very tactful fighter. Her resentment expressed itself too openly, and once when they were all together at the Vale, a quarrel broke out between her and Mrs. Godwin, a quarrel so violent that the distracted object of the strife pushed both women out of the house to settle their differences in the street. Fortunately, the Vale was very private, but Maud broke a blood-vessel, and Whistler was compelled to run for the doctor. Their life together never recovered its equilibrium, and a semicomic incident brought their relationship to an end.

Maud, left alone by Whistler, began to spend her time with her friends, the Stotts. William Stott, "of Oldham," was one of Whistler's followers, and being in need of a model he asked Maud to pose for him. As posing was, or had been, her profession, she consented, and Stott painted from her a large "Venus" or "Nymph," which he sent to the exhibition of the British Artists in Suffolk Street. To the same exhibition Whistler sent a portrait of Maud in bonnet and furs, and this was shown in an adjoining room. Unfortunately, it was obvious that both pictures had been painted from the same model, and as Maud was known to be Whistler's mistress, the incident gave rise to an amount of amusement and curiosity which Whistler found particularly unpleasant. Maud took refuge from his wrath with the Stotts, and soon afterwards Whistler asked Beatrice Godwin to be his wife. She consented, but the marriage might have been postponed indefinitely had it not been for the efforts of their mutual friends. Whistler rushed round to tell Mrs. Jopling-Rowe, and that lady proposed a dinner-party to celebrate the event. The place chosen was the Welcome Club at the Earl's Court Exhibition, and the Labouchères were also invited. Mrs. Rowe announced that she was leaving town at the end of the week and would be glad to see Whistler married before she went. Labouchère made him name the day, and promised to get a clergyman to perform the ceremony. Rowe procured a special license, and Labouchère gave the bride away. Whistler was married to Mrs. Godwin on August 11, 1888, at St. Mary Abbott's, Kensington. He was extremely nervous and anxious to get the ceremony over as soon as possible, fearing some demonstration of protest by Maud. Maud made no sign, but she never forgave

Whistler for his desertion. So far as we know, they never met again. Another chapter in the master's life was closed.

Whistler was now fifty-four, the age at which those who have known many people and have done their own best work, begin to think of writing their reminiscences.[2] Whistler approached the matter with characteristic originality. Most reminiscences are records of friendship; his should be a record of the friends he had shaken off. He resolved to write nothing new, but merely to collect what he had written already. His witty notes, his letters to the papers, his comments in catalogues were to be printed with passages carefully selected from the writings of others.

He discussed the matter with an American journalist, Sheridan Ford, and Ford, with a flash of real inspiration, proposed that the collection should be called "The Gentle Art of Making Enemies." There have been so many "Gentle Arts" since that the title no longer sounds particularly original, but it was a real find when first thought of. It had a flavor of knight-errantry about it that appealed to Whistler, and the sting in its tail delighted him.

It was to be the record of his quarrels, and it was perhaps inevitable that it should be the cause of a quarrel itself. Sheridan Ford, poor misguided man, invented the title, collected the material and got the book ready for the press. He looked to it to make his reputation, but no one made a reputation out of Whistler. Whistler made sure of that.

[2] This is no longer true. The accepted age is now twenty-four.

[ 243 ]

At the last moment he threw his collaborator overboard, withdrew his authorization and proposed to produce the book himself. The work was ready for printing and the type set up, when Messrs. Field and Tuer, the printers, received a warning from Whistler's solicitors that publication would not be permitted. Sheridan Ford, in despair at seeing his labor wasted, had the book set up again in America, but again Whistler's agents intervened.

Ford tried to have it published in Belgium, and an edition of two thousand copies was ready for delivery when they were seized by the Procureur du Roi. "Under the nose of the astounded and discomfited speculator, the packed and corded bales, of which he was about to take possession, were carried off in the government van! The upshot of the untiring efforts of this persistent adventurer at length results in furnishing Mr. Whistler with the first and only copy of this curious work." [3] Ford made a final attempt in Paris and, again frustrated, disappeared into obscurity.

It is impossible not to feel a little sorry for Sheridan Ford, but for Whistler it was a lucky escape. The preface and accessory comments were "in the worst style of western editorship," and the printing was not of the standard he required in a book of his. It is not always realized how important Whistler was as an innovator in typography, as in so much else. He "framed" his print as carefully as he framed his pictures, and as simply, by the use of wide

[3] *Sunday Times,* March 30, 1890.

[ 244 ]

white margins. He may be said to have invented the asymmetrical arrangement of a title-page. He took infinite pains over the printing. Every comma was considered, not only for its position in the sentence but for its place on the page, and at the end of every letter he placed a butterfly with a sting in its tail carefully drawn to accord with the mood of the text. Those who doubt Whistler's meticulous craftsmanship should look through "The Gentle Art," noting only the differing forms of the scorpion-butterfly. It is frivolous, it is ironic, it pounces, it points, it sniggers; it is calm at the foot of the "Propositions," casually contemptuous with Tom Taylor and gathers itself together to transfix P. G. Hamerton with a deadly malignity; it reposes half defiantly, half dejectedly, on the farthing damages of the Ruskin trial, and on the last page of it all it soars above the clouds with the light-heartedness of one whose work is done. Whistler was one of the first to revive the forgotten doctrine that a book should be a work of art which is not finished when the author has scribbled the last page of the manuscript.

"The Gentle Art of Making Enemies" was the story of Whistler's life in London, and he tossed it to the London public as a final gesture, for his thoughts were turning once more to France.

## CHAPTER IX

WHISTLER, in the early seventies, seemed to have dropped out of the consciousness of the French people as completely as he had disappeared from Fantin's pictures. None of his work was to be seen in France and if he survived at all it was as an eccentric memory. The recollection of his wit and his pugnacity lingered on in a limited circle, but a legend is not a reputation. Zola, prompted by Guillemet, was slowly building up the fame of Manet, of whom Whistler in his time had thought and said many uncomplimentary things.

It is hardly necessary to insist upon the insularity (perhaps the pardonable insularity) of the French in all artistic matters. Not to exhibit in Paris is a certificate of oblivion, for French appreciation of what is being done abroad is rarely more than perfunctory. But even had Whistler been known during the years of his eclipse, it is extremely doubtful whether he would have been more appreciated than he was in London. An artist who goes his own way and fails to remain in the vanguard of a movement must not expect recognition in the middle period between his early promise and his later indubitable achievement.

[ 246 ]

However, Whistler had not forgotten Paris nor the sensation he had once caused in the *Salon des Refusés*. When London turned its back upon him after the Ruskin trial he began once more to send his pictures abroad, and his friend Théodore Duret did him immense service in France by his readiness to appraise his work in French art journals. In January, 1879, the Gazette des Beaux-Arts, then very influential, gave an account of the Ruskin trial, and in 1881 the same journal devoted an article to Whistler with especial reference to the etchings brought back from Venice, and to the nocturnes. "Mr. Whistler's nocturnes," said Duret, "make one think of those Wagnerian compositions in which the harmonic sound, separated from all melodic design and any accented cadence, remains a kind of abstraction and conveys only a very indefinite musical impression." [1] In the early eighties to compare Whistler to Wagner was to proclaim his part in the modern intellectual movement and to rally to his side all those to whom the name of Wagner was a battle-cry. Whistler had fallen out of one movement, but he was finding himself caught up in the swell of another.

During the eighties Whistler was a fairly constant exhibitor at the Paris Salon. Both the "Mother" and the "Carlyle" had been shown there as well as his other masterpiece "Miss Alexander," and the portraits of Lady Meux, M. Duret, Lady Archibald Campbell, and Sarasate. Dif-

[1] Gazette des Beaux-Arts, XXIII (1881), p. 368.

ferent as his work was from that of the now accepted school of the impressionists, far as he had drifted from the men with whom his student days had been passed, the French were beginning to see in him a distinguished foreign artist whose work would not be out of place in the Luxembourg.

In 1891 the picture of his mother was exposed for sale in the gallery of a Parisian dealer, and Clemenceau, even then an influential figure, induced the Ministre des Beaux-Arts to purchase it for the nation. With this honor Whistler received another, even more welcome: he was made an officer of the Legion of Honor.

He was accepted! and in Paris, the Paris of his early struggles, while London remained for the most part obstinately unappreciative. Whistler began to wonder whether after all he had not made a mistake in settling in London. He had revealed its beauty to its inhabitants, but they had failed to like his work. He began to toy with the notion of leaving London forever and returning to the French capital where people knew how to value artists.

Even in London, however, his reputation was beginning to emerge from the mists of controversy, although it was not London which paid him the compliment of buying one of his pictures for exhibition in a public gallery. The "Carlyle" had been shown at the Glasgow Institute in 1888, and a movement was begun to purchase it for the city. The price asked was a thousand guineas, six hundred guineas more than it could have been purchased for a year before, and there was a certain amount of opposition from those who thought that to buy pictures, especially Whistler's, was "a piece of wasteful extravagance." However, the Art Club presented to the corporation a memorial signed by over ninety artists and others, and as the corporation had some four thousand pounds in hand it was agreed to purchase the "Carlyle." It was hoped, however, to obtain it for less than a thousand guineas, and two representatives of the corporation—Robert Crawford, chairman of the galleries committee, and "a municipal colleague somewhat Philistine in matters of Art, hard of jaw and straight in speech, whose mission was to 'squeeze' down the price" [2] —came to London to negotiate.

"Mr. Whistler," relates Crawford, "received us with great ceremonial, cordiality, and impressiveness. He wore, *inter alia,* a brown velveteen jacket and loose necktie, with hanging ends, reminiscent of the Boul' Mich'. His hair was oiled and curled and worn well down toward the shoulder. He walked as if on his tiptoes—his head daintily turned sideways, while his bright sparkling eyes and his general air of elegance and grace somehow suggested to us the aspect of a canary or a love-bird."

The love-bird, however, proved more wily than the ambassadors from Glasgow had expected. He gave them

[2] These amusing particulars are taken from an article by Robert Crawford—"How We Bought the Whistler 'Carlyle' "—which appeared in the Glasgow Evening News, March 23, 1905.

"Vienna tea" with lemon and rum in it, and talked brilliantly—about everything but the business in hand. His visitors tried to bring him back to the picture, and Whistler cried:

"The picture; yes, of course, the picture is yours. The great Corporation of Glasgow—most enlightened and humane—most liberal in its ideas—certainly into no better hands can I desire to see my 'Carlyle' placed."

Crawford protested that it was by no means certain that the corporation could afford to pay a thousand guineas. Would eight hundred guineas—

"My dear, ruddy-faced Scot," interrupted Whistler, "what is this we are doing? You and I will never condescend to haggle about money. If it was in my power to bestow this picture on the people of Glasgow as a gift I would gladly do so, as a proof of my appreciation of their good judgment in desiring to possess it. They do so choose, do they not? Alas! I cannot make it a gift, and I wish you to have it. What need, then, to discuss the question of money? But you have not yet seen the picture. It is not here—tomorrow will you give me the felicity to see you again and I will show you the 'Carlyle'?"

As the two visitors were leaving, the "Philistine friend," feeling that he was not playing his part at all well, ventured to suggest that modern pictures were inclined to fade. Whistler threw up his hands. "No," he cried, "they do not fade, and therein lies their complete damnation!"

Next day the two from Glasgow presented themselves again, determined to come straight to the point. "Now, Mr. Whistler, have you, since we saw you yesterday, thought any more about the price of the 'Carlyle'?"

"My dear friends, most estimable of Scotchmen," replied Whistler, "I have, indeed, been thinking, but only on the anticipation of again seeing you this afternoon, after our delightful chat of yesterday—and now that you are here let us talk, smoke, drink tea, and be happy."

The picture was displayed on an easel, and the two prospective buyers looked at it long and critically, racking their brains for something to say. At length the Philistine said: "Mr. Whistler, do you call this life size?"

"No, I don't," snapped Whistler, "there is no such thing as 'life size.' If I put you up against that canvas and measured you, you would be a monster."

The poor bewildered man made one more effort. "The tones of this portrait," he said, "are rather dull, are they not? Not very brilliant, are they?"

Whistler danced. "Not brilliant! No; why should they be?—Are you brilliant? No! Am I brilliant? Not at all! We are not 'highly colored,' are we?—We are very very ordinary-looking people. The picture says that, and no more."

There was nothing more to be done. Whistler got his thousand guineas.

[ 251 ]

Early in 1892, an exhibition of his work was arranged at the Goupil Gallery, and the critics were as favorable as they had previously been hostile, although their hostility has been much exaggerated by his partizans, and Whistler's habit of stringing together selected passages gives a very unfair impression of what was actually written. The device is a familiar one when employed to advertise an artist or an author. By judicious suppression it is nearly always possible to turn a lukewarm review into an ecstasy of rapt admiration. The contrary process is equally possible and equally misleading. As long ago as 1867 Colvin had written in the influential Fortnightly Review:

Mr. Whistler is another artist who aims at beauty without realism. No artist's works more completely mystify the average spectator than his. Everyone can perceive his neglect of form, his contempt for executive finish, the apparently slurring method by which he achieves exactly as much as he wishes, and attempts no more; but not everyone can perceive in what his real strength lies, his perfect mastery of the *rapports* of tone and of what Mr. Rossetti calls the "delicate aberrances and intricate haphazards of color." These, and these alone, are what he attempts to seize, whether in his gray and brown studies of shore and harbor or his brilliant and harmonious compositions of Japanese decorative color. That these are artistic successes after their kind is undeniable; but it may fairly be urged that as pictures, as idealization of fact,

[ 252 ]

they lose value by their exclusiveness of aim and one-sidedness of treatment.[3]

The last sentence, quoted by itself, would give an entirely erroneous impression of the tone of the whole criticism, which, written as it was before any of the great portraits had been painted, is yet singularly just and penetrating.

Whistler's treatment of Wedmore was less than fair. Frederick (afterwards Sir Frederick) Wedmore annoyed Whistler profoundly, probably because he was, as a critic, treated with a respect which Whistler thought due to the artist alone. Of Whistler's Venice etchings, Wedmore had written: "They have a merit of their own, and I do not wish to understate it." This Whistler deliberately misquoted as: "They have a merit of their own, and I do not wish to understand it." Wedmore wrote to the Academy to protest, which gave Whistler the opportunity he had been waiting for. In a letter to the World he offered his barbed apology.

Mr. Frederick Wedmore—a critic—one of the wounded—complains that by dexterously substituting "understand" for "understate," I have dealt unfairly by him, and wrongfully rendered his writing. Let me hasten to acknowledge the error, and apologize. My carelessness is culpable, and the misprint without ex-

[3] See "The Colvins and Their Friends," by E. V. Lucas (London, 1928), p. 13.

cuse; for naturally I have all along known, and the typographer should have been duly warned, that with Mr. Wedmore, as with his brethren, it is always a matter of understating, and not at all one of understanding.

The answer to Wedmore was already written when the misquotation was sent to the press. This was playing the game somewhat low down.

Still, some of the things critics really did say of Whistler's work were surprising enough. Whistler collected the most flagrant and printed them in the Goupil catalogue under the bitter title of "The Voice of a People." Life described his "Nocturne in Blue and Gold—Old Battersea Bridge" as "a Farce in Moonshine with half-a-dozen dots." The Era thought " 'Miss Alexander' one of the strangest and most eccentric specimens of portraiture we ever saw," while Punch described it as "a gruesomeness in Gray," and the Artist as a "Rhapsody in Raw Child and Cobwebs."

Faced with such stupidity, we can only share the artist's irritation, and wonder at the blindness which could see nothing in that exquisite canvas, nothing but the portrait of a "bilious young lady . . . looking haughty in a dirty white dress" left "before the colors were dry in a room where chimney-sweeps were at work."

In 1892 the laugh was on Whistler's side, and the exhibition at the Goupil met with almost universal approval.

Whistler understood the importance of the occasion, and took the greatest pains (not that such pains were unusual with him) in arranging his pictures. He exhibited the best of his portraits, the Japanese pictures he had painted in the sixties, early triumphs like "The Music Room," and a group of the long-abused nocturnes. Forty-three pictures were collected, with considerable trouble, from their owners; and Whistler was very indignant when these same owners, thinking that the interest roused by the exhibition would not last, hastened to throw his works into the market.

Crowds thronged the gallery all day, but Whistler would not appear. He could not forget the years of struggle and misunderstanding. The enthusiasm in the gallery moved him to a bitterness even beyond his wont, and he remarked: "Well, you know, they were always pearls I cast before them, and the people were always—well, the same people." He debated the question of sending a season ticket to Ruskin. The general appreciation of his works, although genuine, came too late. He had already decided to leave London forever.

He returned to Paris with the joy of a schoolboy. His affection for London was always subconscious; in his talk he pretended to detest the place, and in the end he persuaded himself that his dislike was real. France, his first European home, had accepted him at last, and made amends for years of neglect by bestowing upon him the ribbon of the Legion of Honor. No decoration could have been more satisfying to the military romanticism of the painter, and he wore the little rosette with legitimate pride. Besides, he was married at last and ready to settle down for good and all. His bohemian life with Jo, his hand-to-mouth existence with Maud, were alike over. There was now a real Mrs. Whistler, and enough money to keep them both in comfort.

He took a studio at 86 rue Notre Dame des Champs and in the exhilaration of finding himself back in Paris, not as a visitor but as a resident, he did not notice or did not care that it was necessary to climb six flights of steep oak stairs in order to get to it. In the opinion of some who knew him at the time the position of his studio shortened his life by several years. His heart was no longer strong, and he found that it was necessary to rest sometimes on a sofa which, fortunately enough, stood on the landing half-way up.

He did not live in the studio, of course, but found a pleasant apartment at 110 rue du Bac. It was near the lively part of Paris yet sufficiently secluded to insure his privacy. A narrow passage between two shops led to a small paved court, picturesquely derelict, with a bronze fountain, which no longer worked, and the remains of a frieze on the surrounding walls. Whistler's front door, of peacock blue, was on the ground floor, and the apartment itself was slightly below that level, for when the door was opened by the grave-faced English servant, the visitor descended several steps into the hall, with the reception room beyond. The reception room was decorated in accordance with Whistler's admirable taste in such matters. The floor was covered with dark blue matting, the walls were paneled blue and white, and the ceiling, to give it height, was painted a lighter shade of blue. From the center hung a Japanese lantern in the form of a net full of shells and seaweed. There was very little furniture, and what there was was light and graceful. On the walls hung two of the master's sketches, for Whistler's principle was still to hang nothing but his own work and not much of that. Over the tall chimney was a pastel Venus and on the grand piano a few etchings were thrown with studied carelessness.

The Whistlers formed a strange but well-assorted pair; Mrs. Whistler still young and Whistler himself growing old but refusing to admit it, his white lock shining defiantly in a mop of hair which, by nature or not, was still jet-black. His hands were as restless as of old, perpetually adjusting the eye-glass with the familiar gesture, the tongue just as quick, the laugh just as strident.

In the corner of the sitting-room stood a little writing table, which would have looked fragile but for the daintiness of the objects placed upon it—a graceful ink-stand, a few slender quills, and several sheets of very small writing paper.

Whistler would come home from the studio, his eyes

full of mischief, sit down at the little table and poise one of
the quills delicately above a sheet of paper. It was here that
he wrote his notes, here he concocted his epigrams, while
Mrs. Whistler looked on in the hope of being able to persuade him to blunt the sting of the messages he was issuing
to the world.

She was of a placid and kindly disposition, with none of
the fiery temperament of Maud. She considered that her
husband's position was now secure and that the days for
controversy were over. It was high time to begin to keep
one's friends. Her somewhat continental style of beauty
fitted well into the Parisian apartment, and Whistler must
really have felt, as he looked round, that he had found a
home at last.

On the far side of the room a door opened into the garden, furnished with a few decrepit seats and bounded by a
high wall, monastic in its severity. There was indeed a con-
vent on the other side of the wall and morning and evening
the inhabitants of 110 rue du Bac could hear a bell calling
the religious to their devotions.[4] Whistler seems to have
liked it; it did not annoy him like the bells in Venice. He
was fond of the garden and would sit in it to make his lithographs. Here, too, Mrs. Whistler gave the chance visitor tea.

[4] It was an establishment of foreign missions, with a garden "whose
shade continued the foliage of the little enclosure whence Whistler, on the
other side of the wall, heard the prayers and canticles of the missionaries,
seemingly bent on exorcising his diabolisms."—"Mallarmé et les Peintres,"
by Henri de Régnier in L'Art Vivant, 1930, p. 307.

Whistler seemed really established at last in the heart of the French capital, yet the France he found in the late eighties was very different from the France he had left in the early sixties. The overconfidence and the false prosperity of the Second Empire had given place to a mood of disillusionment. Romanticism, already almost dead, had been finally dispatched by the disasters of 1870 and 1871, or rather (for the romantic element is immortal) it had been transformed into something else at once more pessimistic and more intangible. The ghost of itself still hovered over the little tables in the boulevard cafés, where painters and poets sat. But the accepted deity of the movement was no longer the sun-god Hugo, but a cynical and disreputable creature, a down-at-heel Silenus, through whose brain floated pale, exquisite visions of nymphs in forest glades. The young men crowded round the table of Verlaine, as the disciples of Socrates had crowded round their master's chair. Verlaine, indeed, looked very like Socrates—Socrates debauched—but no words of calm wisdom fell from his lips. Nothing but harsh laughter and childish obscenity, and then, just when it was least expected, a flash of that interior beauty, a glimpse of that Watteau-like world of which he alone had the key. Then he would scribble a few words on the back of a dirty envelope, while the young men pressed him to speak of his former friend Rimbaud, the marvelous boy who had created a masterpiece at fifteen, and at thirty had thrown all

[ 259 ]

literature behind him to become a merchant in the up-
lands of Abyssinia. These two, and the calm Mallarmé,
from whose ivory tower came the faint strain of an almost
incomprehensible music, were the gods of the new cult,
the members of which called themselves "symbolists."

Whistler's art, which had drifted so far away from the
main current of French painting, was for many reasons
particularly likely to appeal to the littérateurs of the symbolist movement. They were tired of crude colors and fond
of twilight. So was Whistler. Their taste was perfect, but
lacking all robustness. So was his. They delighted in the
suggestion of mystery, in contours lost in shadows, in
figures that emerged from a misty background like the
people of a dream. Whistler's later portraits satisfied all
these requirements. Sometimes a whole school of literature
seems to possess a definite color, and the color of symbolism
is gray-blue, just such a shade as Whistler mixed upon his
palet when he sat down to paint a nocturne.

The first "White Girl," when it was exhibited thirty
years before, had been called a spirit-portrait. To the
symbolists the phrase was a pure compliment. Not for
them the crude flesh of a Rubens, the massive muscularity
of a Michelangelo. They required no more than a suggestion, a delicate flavor, lest they should jar their exquisite
sensibility. Whistler was as sophisticated as they were themselves, and the fragile, delicate women who emerged from
(nay! hid behind) his canvases, were the victims of an

[ 260 ]

almost morbid overrefinement, fit denizens for the twilight world of the symbolists.

It has been necessary to dwell at some length upon this poetic atmosphere, because of the strange and (in modern eyes) damaging fact that the appreciation which greeted Whistler on his return to France was almost entirely a literary appreciation.

J. K. Huysmans wrote:

> Inevitably one thought of De Quincey's visions, of those flights of rivers, those fluid dreams opium evokes. In their frame of pallid gold, vermiculate with turquoise-blue and dotted with silver, these air- and waterscapes extended into infinity, suggested thoughts in the balance, magically transported into ages gone never to return, into the illimitable. It was far from modern life, far from everything, at the outmost bounds of painting, that seemed to evaporate in an invisible smoke of colors, on these fragile canvases.

Huysmans also wrote of "this shadow incarnated in the twofold shape of a woman tangible and at the same time fluid," which he perceived in Whistler's feminine portraits: "those phantom portraits that seemed to retreat, to try to thrust themselves into the wall, with their enigmatic eyes and their mouths an icy, ghoulish red."

Whistler, in the eyes of Huysmans, was the master most in tune with the spirit of the time, and his art "a convalescent, exquisite, altogether personal, utterly new painting." In a sense he was right, but in what other period would the adjective *convalescente* have seemed a word of praise? The writer goes on to compare him with Verlaine, for the poet had pushed poetry to the confines of music, and the painter had pushed painting to the verge of literature. In the mouth of a modern critic there could be no deadlier insult.

Of the three pillars of the symbolist movement (although such groupings are in general no more than convenient tags) Rimbaud, as we have seen, had vanished from the Paris boulevards. Verlaine, with his squalid habits and repulsive appearance, was the last man in the world to attract the fastidious Whistler, who, moreover, cared almost nothing for literature. Mallarmé was very different. He was both cultivated and clean, and, best of all, admired Whistler's painting, whether or no he thought that it had any connection with his own artistic ideals. Mallarmé was a teacher of English and had lived for a time in England in order to prepare himself for his post by study of the language and literature. Baudelaire's translation of Edgar Allan Poe drew his attention to the works of that writer which still awaited rendering into French. He undertook the task himself, and then (for Whistler, like Poe, was an American with a touch of diabolism) he translated Whistler's "Ten o'Clock." So high a compliment paid by one writer to another could not fail to lead to a better acquaintance. In the words of Henri de Régnier, who knew

Mallarmé well: "Between poet and painter there came about a veritable 'thunderbolt' of cordiality and understanding."[5] The return of Whistler to Paris was marked by a flash of his old genius for making friends.

The two men met soon after the painter's return to Paris, before Whistler had moved his belongings into the apartment in the rue du Bac, and when he was staying at the Hôtel du Bon Lafontaine. Pennell found them together in Whistler's bedroom, Mallarmé sitting for the lithograph portrait which was afterwards used as the frontispiece to his works.

Whistler could not have made a more agreeable acquaintance, for Mallarmé was in touch with most of the writers and artists of the "advanced" schools. He was a close friend of the Manets, especially of Berthe Morizot (Madame Eugène Manet), and to his "Tuesdays" came artists as dissimilar as Odilon Redon, grave-faced and shy, and the uproarious Gauguin, with his massive body clothed in a sailor's jersey, his enormous hands and his raucous voice, on a chance visit to Mallarmé between two voyages to Tahiti. Mallarmé invited Whistler to a "Tuesday" to hear a reading of his translation of the "Ten o'Clock." When it was published in Edouard Dujardin's Revue Indépendante it had created great interest, and there was a good attendance of friends to hear it read.

[5] "Mallarmé et les Peintres," by Henri de Régnier in L'Art Vivant, 1930, p. 308.

When all was ready, Mallarmé began to read, his soft but distinct voice murmuring Whistler's phrases, transmuted and transfigured by the magic of another language. There is a curious pleasure for any writer in good translations of his own works. To be translated into French is to think oneself witty, and to be translated into German is to know oneself learned. The "Ten o'Clock" was, of course, witty already, and Mallarmé was a translator of genius. Few evenings of his existence could have given Whistler greater pleasure. Here was recognition indeed! Yet, once again, a literary recognition.

It is true that he was not ignored as a painter. His work was well hung in the Salon of 1892, and he was elected a *Sociétaire* and a member of the jury. But the painting of his maturity could never cause quite the sensation that the first "White Girl" had caused almost a lifetime before, and Whistler may well have felt that it was less honor for his work to be on exhibition in the Salon of 1892 than in the *Salon des Refusés* of 1863.

It must sometimes have been borne in upon him that French art had gone its own way, and that that way was not his. Writers and dandies like Octave Mirbeau and the Comte de Montesquiou came to see him, but not many painters. Why should they? Painters, especially French painters, are not often distinguished by the breadth of their artistic sympathy. Many of them probably regarded him, if they thought about him at all, as a distinguished foreign painter; but why should they be interested in foreign painters, however distinguished? There could be no question of discipleship, for Whistler and they had almost nothing in common.

It was also true—and Whistler must have felt this acutely—that his personal prestige counted for almost nothing in Paris. Had he been ten times as eccentric as he was, he would still have passed unnoticed, and Whistler later in life had refined away the earlier licenses of his attire until eccentricity was swallowed up in dandyism. Moreover, Whistler's peculiar talents needed a social background, and this was lacking in Paris, for French hostesses do not lionize. The gulf between society and bohemia is not to be crossed so easily, partly because French bohemians are real bohemians, not diners-out in fancy dress.

Whistler, therefore, was not courted, although he had his own court and knew how to shine in it. But his courtiers were, almost without exception, Anglo-Saxons. In England he was still looked upon as the chief rebel against academic art, and every progressive young painter passing through Paris was eager to call upon him. Lavery came, and Sargent, Beardsley and Jacomb-Hood and James Guthrie, and a great many artists from the United States, for Whistler was no longer without honor in his own country. American collectors began to seek him out, and their deference and their readiness to buy his works compensated him for the neglect of the French. This did not prevent him from suffering the pangs of that "persecution mania" which had grown up during his struggle for recognition and which survived, as it often does, when the struggle was over.

A third cause must be added to those which increased Whistler's isolation among French artists. Mrs. Whistler, in spite of her Latin type of beauty, and in spite of having married two very un-English artists, had her own insular prejudice against the foreigner and, as her French was poor, French artists cannot have felt themselves very welcome. Her influence over Whistler was enormous, and he could not help being affected by her opinions and prejudices. She longed for tranquillity, and almost succeeded in persuading him to write no more of those barbed little notes which gave Whistler such pleasure to concoct, and involved him in so many difficulties afterwards.

Her principal failure was the case of the "Baronet and the Butterfly." This unfortunate interruption to Whistler's work was a sign of his utter lack of proportion. Only men with nothing else to do can afford to have so punctilious a sense of honor. A man with work on hand—a serious artist, in fact—cannot be always taking offense. The fault was not entirely on Whistler's side. The pity is that he wasted so much time in legal proceedings.

The baronet had been introduced to Whistler by George Moore, who was still on friendly terms. Lady Eden had already been painted by several artists, but her husband wished her to be painted by Whistler. Possibly because he had so many pictures already, he thought a pastel or small water-color sketch would be sufficient. The price tentatively agreed upon was a hundred guineas—or a hundred and fifty. It should be mentioned that Sir William had already inquired through Whistler's agents in London what the price of a portrait of his wife would be. The agents suggested five hundred guineas, and it was because the baronet did not wish to spend so much that he got George Moore to introduce him to Whistler, and suggested a water-color sketch.

Commissions of this kind are always dangerous unless the client is willing to allow the artist a certain elasticity. Portraits cannot be ordered at so much per yard, and Whistler, once his work was started, forgot all about money, although as soon as the work was finished he remembered it with some passion. Lady Eden was very beautiful, and Whistler took great pleasure in painting her; so much pleasure, in fact, that the project of a small water-color was abandoned, and a full-length oil painting produced instead.

Both the lady and her husband were pleased with the portrait; but Sir William had ordered a hundred-guinea work, and he had no intention of paying more than a hundred guineas. It seems probable that it was simply lack of imagination on his part which led him to hand Whistler a check for that amount without even asking his opinion.

With a facetiousness singularly misplaced, he enclosed his check in a sealed envelope and handed it to Whistler on St. Valentine's Day, with the remark: "Here is your Valentine. You can open it when I am gone."

Whistler opened it, and his rage can be imagined. He sat down immediately to write one of his terrible little notes. There was no mistaking the tone of Whistler's sarcasm, and Sir William called to demand an explanation. He offered to make the sum up to a hundred and fifty guineas, but Whistler was beyond being pacified. He was not quarreling about money, but on a point of honor.

The conversation between the two men took place on the stairs, as Whistler barred the entrance to his studio. The parting was not friendly. Whistler refused to deliver the portrait, but sent it instead to the exhibition in the Champ-de-Mars. Very foolishly, he cashed Sir William Eden's check.

The baronet continued to demand his portrait, and Whistler at last replied that he preferred to refund the money rather than let Sir William have the picture. Meanwhile, he scraped out the head to make certain that no portrait of Lady Eden should remain to be bargained for.

Sir William entered legal proceedings against Whistler, and the case was tried in Paris before the civil tribunal, at the end of February, 1895. The trial makes very dull reading, for there were no nocturnes or Titians to bring into court as in the Ruskin libel action. The court decided hat Whistler had put himself in the wrong, and he was condemned to refund the hundred guineas, to deliver up he portrait as it was and, in addition, to pay a thousand rancs damages for Lady Eden's expenses while she had been in Paris. Whistler was outraged by this judgment and at once appealed to the Cour de Cassation. Pennell tried to raise a fund to pay his expenses, and records bitterly in his life of Whistler that only one contribution was received. His disappointment was natural, but the accusation he brings against artists in England of being "afraid" to support Whistler, is nonsense. To put it mildly, it was by no means certain that Whistler was right. Many artists were more friendly with Sir William Eden than they were with Whistler, and even if they had not been, the man who was prepared to back Whistler in every quarrel needed not only infinite patience but infinite leisure.

Whistler, irritated by the general disapproval, became more and more extravagant. The New English Art Club hung some of Sir William Eden's own work—nor is it easy to see why they should not have done so, if a thousand Whistlers had quarreled with him. The relative greatness of the two men has less than nothing to do with it. But Whistler hurled the word "toad" at them singly and collectively, and when he came to draw up his account of the proceedings in the little pamphlet called "The Baronet and the Butterfly," he printed a toad on the title-page, with the dedication: "To those *confrères* across the Channel who, refraining from intrusive demonstration with a pluck and delicacy all their own, 'sat tight' during the struggle these decrees of the judges are affectionately dedicated.' Whistler really expected English artists to rush over to Paris to help him, but how they could have done so is not easy to see, since they would not have been allowed to appear as witnesses.

A follower who did not break off his friendly relationship with Sir William received a card with "Judas Iscariot" written upon it. George Moore, who had introduced his friend to Whistler, was sent an insulting letter, and when he replied Whistler challenged him to a duel. On Whistler's side everything was in order; seconds were appointed (one of them was Octave Mirbeau) and all arrangements made; but Moore very sensibly ignored the challenge, and Whistler's martial ardor had to remain unsatisfied.

As if he had not enough on his hands already, Whistler became involved in an action brought by Joseph Pennell against Walter Sickert. The latter, in an article in the Saturday Review, had criticized the Pennell exhibition of lithographs at the Fine Arts Society. The inconvenience of lithography consists in the fact that the process involves the use of a very heavy stone. The etcher can carry his grounded plates in his pocket; the really conscientious lithographer from nature needs a truck. The difficulty is surmounted by using lithographic paper from which the

[ 270 ]

design is transferred to the stone in the artist's studio. Only so could Pennell's rapid transcriptions of scenery and architecture all over Europe be made possible at all.

Sickert, in his article, adopted the purist view that Pennell's work was not true lithography, and Pennell, as combative as Whistler himself, brought an action for libel. When the time came for the trial, Whistler, harassed by other troubles, would have been glad to avoid being called upon as a witness. He preferred to be a principal in any fight that was toward. But he had written the introduction to Pennell's catalogue, and had himself used transfer paper for his lithographs. Pennell appealed to him not to desert a cause which concerned them both, and Whistler appeared as his chief witness.

He had already broken with Sickert, once his most constant follower, and the case gave him an opportunity of snubbing him publicly. He referred to him as "an absolutely unknown authority," and "an insignificant and irresponsible person." The plaintiff was awarded fifty pounds damages. Whistler was more successful on Pennell's behalf than he had been on his own.

His own interest in lithography was of long standing. Way, the lithographer, had bought one of his pastels while he was at work on the Peacock Room, and Godwin brought the two men together. Way never lost an opportunity of urging the use of lithography upon his artist friends, and Whistler was persuaded by him to experiment. Whistler

[ 271 ]

had a stone sent to his studio, and Maud posed for him standing in a flowered hat and a long skirt with a train which she gathered up in her right hand. Whistler's first attempt at lithography was extraordinarily successful. He used, the younger Way tells us, "the whole gamut of the chalks provided. The face and many parts of the figure seem to have been drawn with a firm, hard chalk, and then as he could not readily get sufficient color from it, he had tried another of a softer kind, and wound up with a chalk known as *crayon estompe,* almost too soft to draw with at all, and intended to be applied with a stump—indeed there is a suggestion of delicate stumping on the face and hair—finishing up by scraping away some of the superfluous and intense blackness which the last chalk would give." [6]

Whistler took up the process with such enthusiasm— urged thereto also by the state of his finances—that he had produced seventeen lithographs before leaving for Venice. He took some transfer paper with him, but was too busy with his etchings and pastels to work in the other medium and, even after his return, he found so much to occupy his time that it was not until 1887 that he turned to lithography again. Transfer paper had been much improved in the interval, and he was able to take a little packet of it about with him, even more conveniently than he could

[6] "Memories of James McNeill Whistler," by T. R. Way (London 1912), p. 8.

carry copperplates. He used the process in his studio also for rapid sketches from the nude model, and some of these studies are among the most exquisite of his productions. Encouraged by Way, he began to experiment with colored lithography, but the results at first were not so happy.

Mrs. Whistler's enthusiasm for lithography caused her husband to take it up again, and the greater part of his lithographic work was done during the few years he lived with her in Paris. He made a whole series of prints of the Luxembourg Gardens, as well as portraits of Mallarmé and Count Robert de Montesquiou.

It was in 1894 that Mrs. Whistler's health began to break down, and Whistler was too distracted to work. Lithography, however, he tried to keep up, for he could work at it while seated at her bedside. He stayed with her at Lyme Regis, and wrote to Way to make the necessary preparations for printing his work. He even arranged for an exhibition of his lithographs to be held at the Fine Art Society's Galleries. There were sixteen in all, done at Lyme Regis; six of them showing the interior of forges and smithies, a subject he had treated years before in etching but never attempted in lithography.

In 1895 he lived in London, more and more anxious about his wife. At Long's Hotel, in Bond Street, he began a portrait of Lady Haden, and from the De Vere Hotel he made a drawing of Kensington Gardens. He also produced drawings of the Pennells and the elder Way. He was so

[ 273 ]

restless that he could not sit down, yet so tired with watching beside Mrs. Whistler's bed that he sometimes fell asleep over the lithographic stone.

Mrs. Whistler's health grew worse and worse, and she was removed to rooms at the Savoy Hotel, high up, and looking over the river. Here he made a most moving drawing of the sick woman in bed, but insisted on calling it "The Siesta," in a pathetic attempt to persuade himself that such indeed it was. This, and the views of London from the hotel windows, are among the finest of all his prints. The lithotint, "The Thames," is one of the masterpieces of lithography.

He was to make very few more lithographs. Mrs. Whistler was dying of cancer, and it became necessary to move her from the Savoy to a nursing home on Hampstead Heath, and there, on May 10, 1896, she died. A friend met him on that day, running wildly across the Heath, his dress for once disordered, his hair flying in the wind.

"Don't speak to me," he cried. "Don't speak to me," and fled.

## CHAPTER X

### THE LAST YEARS

WHISTLER was fond of declaring that the artist has no roots, no relation to his time or country. However untrue this may be of most artists, including the greatest, there was an element of truth in it when applied to himself, for it was his nature to take root nowhere. Wherever he went he was always the foreigner, and it may be conjectured that he would have seemed no less so even if he had returned to America as, once or twice, he half thought of doing. He had made several attempts to settle down, once when he built the White House, and once when he took the apartment in the rue du Bac. On both occasions his home was broken up, the first by his bankruptcy, the second by the death of his wife.

After his bereavement he was a pathetic figure and seemed quite unable to make up his mind where to go. He lived for a time with his wife's sister and mother in Hampstead, but he knew that it was only for a time. He was restless and homeless. The Eden affair was still dragging on, and he knew that he would have to attend the Paris court sooner or later. At last the case was retried before the Cour de Cassation. The superior court reaffirmed

[ 275 ]

the first judgment: that Whistler was to refund Sir William Eden's hundred guineas and pay one thousand francs damages but Whistler was allowed to keep the portrait on condition that it was made unrecognizable. This, as we have seen, had already been done. Whistler paid the costs of the first trial, and Sir William the costs of the appeal.

The delight of Whistler seems out of all proportion to the extent of his triumph. He declared that the trial had "made history," added a new clause to the Code Napoléon and vindicated his honor before all Paris. He determined to make a book of the affair, and did so, but it was a failure. Nobody seemed to be interested in "The Baronet and the Butterfly."

Whistler began to feel that he was losing ground. He was more famous than he had ever been, but in less personal a fashion. His appearance no longer created the excitement it had caused in the eighties. As his personality had once obscured his painting, so his painting now eclipsed his personality. One cannot be both old master and young rebel. The fashionable world, avid for novelty, had found new idols. The esthetes had changed into decadents, and Blue and White China, real or imitation, was now too common to excite remark. It had been a mistake to go to Paris. Once more he had fallen out of the "Movement."

He made journeys to some of the smaller English towns —Rochester, Canterbury, Whitby—and produced a few water-colors; but his heart was not in the work, and the English climate was unfriendly. He began to feel himself an old man (when his wife died he was sixty-two) and his skill in ridding himself of "the friendship of the many" had left him rather lonely. He was the more grateful for an unexpected companionship.

William Heinemann, founder of the publishing house of that name, was much attracted by Whistler, and he had sufficient tact to keep the master's regard. He had a flat in Whitehall Court and invited Whistler to take up his quarters there. The arrangement gave Whistler a home in London without the responsibilities of a household, and he lived there until Heinemann's marriage, and even a little after.

He always hoped to return to Paris, and, unwilling to give up his apartment in the rue du Bac, he established his wife's relations, Mrs. and Miss Birnie Philip, there to keep house for him. He even retained the studio with its exhausting stairs.

As an artist he was now accepted in London, and the great fight of his life was over. His reputation had been established by the exhibition of 1892, and in the late nineties probably stood higher than it has stood since. But he lacked the power, possessed by so many rebels, of meeting recognition with benevolence. It had come too late. He was compelled to go on fighting, and since his cause had been won the quarrels of his latter years take on an unfortunate appearance of personal pique. He never forgave the British public, and his resentment hardened into a sarcastic contempt of everything English.

He made savage fun of the preparations to celebrate Queen Victoria's Jubilee, finding in them something characteristic of the complacent stupidity of the "Islanders," and apparently oblivious of the fact that England is one of the few countries where public functions retain a certain dignity. He should have been grateful for the chains of office and the bright uniforms. Perhaps he had never seen a French mayor in frock coat and tricolor sash. But he was determined that everything the English did should be ridiculous, and he had no difficulty in finding it so.

This prejudice was nowhere more apparent than in his attitude toward the war in South Africa. As a West Pointer he felt a proprietary interest in all wars, and as an incurable romantic he thought he knew how they ought to be conducted. They should be picturesque affairs—a marching to battle with banners waving, to be followed by the scene of one elegant commander surrendering his sword to another. The Spanish-American War appealed to his imagination. The Americans were heroes and the Spaniards gentlemen. Had he not fought against them himself on the stricken field of Valparaiso? An American officer in London after the war mentioned some of the blunders which, as he quite rightly remarked, were inevitable in any war. Whistler would have none of it. The mere thought was treason to West Point. Only the British made blunders.

[ 278 ]

He searched the papers eagerly for news of British disasters. He even made collections of cuttings and sent them round to his friends. His bitter remarks made him the center of a hostile eddy at every dinner party. Occasionally the old wit leaps out, as when in answer to Buller's recorded boast that he had retreated without losing a man or a gun, he replied: "Yes, or a minute." But many of his sallies were merely ill-natured. Long-suffering as the English were in these matters, it is not surprising that Whistler's popularity did not increase.

His fame as an artist was too well established to be shaken. On his return to Paris after the Sickert lawsuit, he found Boldini anxious to paint him, and Helleu to etch his portrait while he sat to Boldini. The Boldini picture is as hard and merciless as a photograph. A Whistler without charm, contorted into a conscious pose, eye-glass in place, twisted fingers touching the head, stares irritable defiance at the world. The advance of age only increased his exasperation against those he had wasted his time in fighting when he might have been painting masterpieces.

He had avoided middle age by refusing to notice it. In his endeavor to be young still, there was something as pathetic as the efforts of a fading beauty. What became of the famous white lock if the whole head was gray? He tried hard to rejuvenate his appearance. He even painted his cheeks, and his clothes were carefully chosen to emphasize the elegance of his still youthful figure. "This devil of a man, noisy in public, a chatterbox, childishly vain, wanted to cheat himself . . . Jimmie still wishes to be a dandy *à la d'Aurevilly*." [1]

While he was sitting to Boldini, a young Austrian, Josef Engelhart, visited him in an endeavor to secure his support of the Vienna Secession. He has left a vivid account of Whistler, whom he describes as a dainty little doll-like man in a gray frock coat; in his right hand a gray top-hat, in his left a fragile cane, black dancing pumps on his small feet, and of course the inevitable monocle perpetually adjusted with a nervous hand. He reminded Engelhart of a marionette or of some fantastic figure out of the "Tales of Hoffmann." Other visitors described him as looking like an old conjurer, perpetually making mesmeric passes with his fragile hands; and the landlady of an inn at Poole when, with his eternal craving to be noticed, he asked her who or what she thought he was, replied: "I should fancy you was from the 'Alls."

He asked Engelhart what other artists had promised to join Secession, and the young man mentioned a few—Puvis de Chavannes, Besnard, Thaulow.

"Have you got Degas?" snapped Whistler. "You must have Degas. That is essential. So far as painting goes, there's only Degas and myself." This high estimate of Degas was at least partly inspired by Whistler's wholesome respect for his devastating wit. But Degas was very hard to "get," and Engelhart retired discomfited. Next time he

[1] "De David à Degas," by Jacques Emile Blanche (Paris, 1909), p. 67.

WHISTLER IN 1870: *By Charles Keene. In the possession of Lt. Col. Christopher Heseltine.*

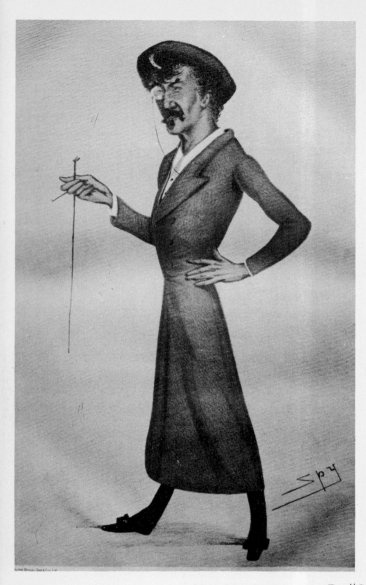

WHISTLER IN 1878: *By "Spy" (Sir Leslie Ward). Vanity Fair, XIX, p. 22.*

was in England he told the story to Lavery, and was shrewdly advised to read "The Gentle Art of Making Enemies" and to quote it in Whistler's presence as a prelude to making friends.

Engelhart had no time to read "The Gentle Art" before he left for Paris next day, but he resolved to call upon the author and make one more attempt to obtain a picture for the Vienna exhibition.

Visitors were becoming a nuisance in the rue du Bac, and Whistler received him none too graciously. "Are you a dealer?" he asked. When reminded of the meeting in Boldini's studio he said, "Oh, yes, you want to get some pictures out of me?"

"Not at all," was the cunning reply. "I have just come from England where I have been reading your famous book, 'The Gentle Art of Making Enemies,' and I felt I must come directly I arrived in Paris to express my admiration."

The hard eyes softened, the painted cheeks relaxed into a smile, Engelhart was invited in, shown all over the apartment, asked to stay to a meal. And he got his pictures. Whistler still lived in the smell of battle, and the field of victory meant more to him than the conquered province.

International exhibitions were "in the air," and even in England a group of artists was endeavoring to found the "International Society of Sculptors, Painters and Gravers." It was natural that Whistler, the "cosmopolitan artist," should be chosen as its first president. He was delighted. Here was no old ship like the British Artists, on the rocks already and with the crew in mutiny, but a brand-new craft, with himself as captain. He insisted that the constitution should be as autocratic as possible, and his name was of infinite value in persuading foreign artists to lend their work. The skating rink in Knightsbridge—now a garage—was fitted up to house the pictures, and the first venture was a great success, except financially.

The painter Anthony Ludovici made a journey to Paris in order to collect work for the exhibition. He found Whistler "laid up with an influenza cold, wrapped in flannel, inhaling eucalyptus from a steaming jug"; but his interest was active, and a list was drawn up of artists who should be asked to contribute. Degas refused to have anything to do with it, but Rodin was affable, and a meeting with Whistler was arranged. Besnard, when consulted, advised Whistler and Ludovici to go to a certain painter called Cézanne, who was beginning to be talked of in the studios. Whistler disliked all Cézanne's pictures, and pointing to one of them said: "If a child of ten had drawn that on her slate, her mother, if she had been a good mother, ought to have slapped her." Ludovici persuaded him to allow a small landscape and a small still life of Cézanne's to be shown in London. Whistler could never have guessed that the works of this despised artist would one day have a greater influence than his own.

[ 282 ]

The International Society was not his only activity in the late nineties. He thought at one time of turning himself into a financial firm, a kind of "Whistler Limited" or "Whistler Inc." to be called "The Company of the Butterfly." The profits of the middleman were to be eliminated. A gallery was taken and an exhibition held, but there were few visitors, and the project came to nothing.

He bethought himself of an earlier ambition. In the autumn of 1898 was announced the opening of a school, at first called the Académie Whistler, but better known as the Académie Carmen from the name of Whistler's model. Madame Carmen, a massive but handsome woman with black hair and dark eyes, took a large studio in the Passage Stanislas, off the rue Notre-Dame-des-Champs and Whistler authorized her to announce that he would view the work of the students twice a week. The sculptor, MacMonnies, was to be the other visiting professor.

Whistler was regarded with idolatrous veneration by many of the young American and English girls studying art, or pretending to study art, in Paris. They followed him in the street, asked him for his autograph, even begged to be allowed to sit for him as models, and when it was announced that he intended to teach at the Académie Carmen, the studio was choked with eager young women, some of whom came with servants and carriages, and dressed as for Longchamps.

Whistler delayed his arrival until the pupils had got

over their first excitement. Then he made a "star entrance," exquisitely dressed as ever, and passed rapidly round glancing, not at the easels, but at the palets. His theory was that a correct palet was three-quarters of the battle. He arranged a palet to show how it was done.

MacMonnies, coming in a few days later, found all the pupils painting mulattoes. He looked at the model. Her skin was particularly white. Evidently there had been some misunderstanding of the master's lesson. The truth seems to be that Whistler had no gift for teaching at all. His methods were too individual to be transmitted, and the element of chance in his own work too great to make him a good example. His manner was the reverse of tactful; he was very authoritative; he segregated the sexes and forbade smoking. The pupils who had hoped for a short cut to fame began to drift away. Soon the men's class had ceased to exist, and the women's did not long survive it. Two faithful pupils were left, and these Whistler bound to himself by "Articles of Apprenticeship"—a meaningless, but gallant gesture of protest against a world from which the tradition of painting, the age-long relationship of master and pupil, had departed.

Whistler's own work was beginning to show, not so much a failing, as a shrinking, of power. He essayed easier subjects, confined himself to heads or half-length figures, and the poses, never very varied, grew strikingly monotonous. Still, he produced some exquisite things—"The Little

Rose of Lyme Regis," "Lillie in Our Alley," "The Little
Lady Sophie of Soho," full of the wistfulness which he always managed to instil into his studies of young girlhood.
He discovered a beautiful new model, and a fresh enthusiasm for studies of the nude. In the open he worked rapidly
in water-color, seizing evanescent effects of light and
atmosphere.

The strong if fragile-looking body, which had given
him so little trouble in his life, began to show signs of
wearing out. The apartment in the rue du Bac was damp,
and he suffered from perpetual colds. The stairs up to his
studio were a dangerous strain on his heart. He took an
apartment in a hotel, but was not much better off. The old
zest was gone. He was an old man, and tired. Some of his
early friends he saw again, but not many; they had drifted
too far apart. So much had happened since the days when
Fantin-Latour was the recipient of his every confidence.
He thought of writing his life, and even began the introduction, with a flash of the old fighting spirit:

> Determined that no mendacious scamp shall tell
> the foolish truth about me when centuries have gone
> by, and anxiety no longer pulls at the pen of the
> "pupil" who would sell the soul of his master, I now
> proceed to take the wind out of such speculator by
> immediately furnishing myself the fiction of my own
> biography, which shall remain, and is the story of
> my life.

[ 285 ]

Whistler never wrote easily. His smallest notes were worked upon with infinite care, and the labor was now beyond him. Besides, he had lived so long, made so many friends, so many enemies. Even the effort of a plain narrative appalled him, and he wished to aim at something more than plain narrative.

Heinemann suggested that Henley should write the life, but Whistler did not approve. He feared, rather pathetically, that Henley would be too critical. He resolved to ask the Pennells to undertake the task, and they consented. Pennell was not a man whom most people found it easy to get on with. He had strong prejudices, and a certain truculence which was like Whistler's own but without Whistler's polish. However, he had an unbounded admiration for Whistler and a complete contempt for Whistler's enemies. Whistler decided that he could not be in better hands.

Small quarrels continued to distract him, and unfortunately the reasons for them grew smaller while the irritation they caused him increased. They ceased to possess any background, they were no longer part of the struggle for a cause but the peevishness of an old and exasperated man. Whistler had lived on his nerves too long. Although he no longer used the apartment in the rue du Bac he became fiercely irritated with a neighbor who persisted in shaking her carpet into the little courtyard. His servant captured the carpet, but his lawyer warned him that such high-handed action would never be supported by the

French courts and Whistler was forced to acquiesce in defeat. There was no longer, even, the same pleasure in fighting.

His doctor advised him to seek a warmer climate, but his journey to Algiers and Tangier was disastrous, for the bad weather followed him. He took refuge in Corsica and for the first time in his life rested.

Back in London, he grew tired of living in hotels and took a house in Chelsea, No. 74 Cheyne Walk, a stone's throw from Lindsey Row, where he had first settled so many years before.

The mother and sister of his dead wife kept house for him, but he was not to find peace even there. He was hardly established before building operations started on the house next door, and the tap-tapping of the workmen deprived him of all rest. Such things can be annoying enough at any time of life, even for those in perfect health. To Whistler they were maddening beyond endurance. He consulted his lawyer but was told there was no redress.

In despair he set forth once more on his travels. He had always had a liking for Holland, and now its quiet dignity appealed to him more than ever. With a friend he went to The Hague, and the Queen of Holland sent her own doctor to look after him. He recaptured his old enthusiasm for the Dutch masters, even taking a dangerous journey to Haarlem to gaze at the Frans Hals.

In London again he fitted up his studio and tried to

[ 287 ]

work. There Pennell found him painting a new picture called "The Daughter of Eve." The model was an Irish girl, and her red hair hung over her shoulders. As he painted did he think of that other Irish girl who had come with him to Chelsea nearly half a century before and whose red hair—"not a gilded, but a coppered red"—he had bade her shake loose over her shoulder for the admiration of Courbet. Maud, too, had had red hair, and the slender elegant figure that he loved. He had always loved women, not crudely but for something which it would be pretentious to call their spirituality and an understatement to call their elegance. He had loved them with a tender penetration for which there is no adjective but Whistlerian, and that indicates the unique quality of the world he created. For he did create a world.

It is a curious achievement this creation of a world, for it has no essential connection with the greatest art. We talk of Botticelli's world, of Watteau's, even of Conder's, but not of Michelangelo's. The greatest artists, those that are pictorial artists first and foremost, deal with form and color, as it were, directly, and for their own sake. Some lesser men seem to interpose a veil between our eyes and reality, a veil of poetry which is at once their charm and their limitation. It is not a limitation of subject matter. No painter limited himself in this respect more vigorously than Degas with his perpetual ballet-girls. Yet the poetry of Degas is pictorial in a sense in which Whistler's is not.

Whistler's world is a world of half-lights and dim colors peopled with shadowy figures, each with a fine-cut profile and slender silhouette, half wraith, half woman of the world. In this closed garden from which all grossness is excluded, women are the chief inhabitants, save where a dehumanized Irving appears for a moment dressed as Philip II, or Sarasate, with his violin under his arm, emerges from the enveloping shadows. His most typical women wear the dress of the seventies, a costume which suited well with Whistler's notions of elegance, for the bustle, unlike the crinoline, did not dwarf the feminine figure, did not conceal but emphasized its curves. It was a dress to walk in, and Whistler's women are rarely seated. They are scarcely creatures of flesh and blood at all, yet, in their sophisticated fashion, infinitely seductive. Their life is in their nerves, and it awakens echoes in a sensibility wholly modern, or rather late nineteenth-century, for the present age is an age of crude reactions. They are complete in themselves, for the vision that created them was itself highly individual, distilling its own peculiar poetry for which no other has the receipt. Whistler's world is rounded and unique.

But now it was crumbling about him. In the autumn of 1902 he was constantly ill, unable to go out, bored unless visitors came to see him, quickly tired when he had them. His bed was moved down-stairs into a small room next to the studio, and when he felt strong enough he would

[ 289 ]

emerge clad in a shabby old overcoat—a pathetic protest against the slovenliness of a dressing-gown. He looked painfully fragile, as if his whole body had gone brittle, and so small that the overcoat which had once fitted his dapper figure neatly hung in telltale folds. He kept up the pretense of working, but could accomplish nothing.

He was annoyed by reporters, and not for his own notoriety but for that of a man whom he was painting: Canfield, whose gambling activities supplied the New York press with headlines. Whistler had introduced him to his mother- and sister-in-law and that in his eyes constituted a certificate of gentility. He would hear nothing against him.

He began to plan the issue of a new pamphlet ridiculing Wedmore, but the project came to nothing, in spite of the help of Heinemann. On New Year's Day he sent out to his friends cards signed with the Butterfly. But he must have been conscious that his life was almost over, for he made the final arrangements for the Pennells to write his life and he began to destroy drawings and paintings which he did not think good enough to survive him. Yet he revived the prospect of living with Heinemann again, and the latter took a new flat for the purpose; but Whistler grew steadily feebler and on Friday, July 17, 1903, he died.

Old Chelsea Church was very near his home, and it was there that the funeral service was held on the Wednesday following his death. There was not a large attendance:

a few friends, a few academicians, and the official representatives of the International Society of which he had been
president. In a corner, unnoticed, sat the "White Girl."
More than a generation ago she and Whistler had parted
and she was now an old woman. Yet in "the Mirror"
which the artist had held up to her she was young still.

> Deep in the gleaming glass,
> She sees all past things pass,
> And all sweet life that was lie down and die.
>
> Face fallen and white throat lifted,
> With sleepless eye,
> She sees old loves that drifted,
> She knew not why,
> Old loves and faded fears,
> Float down a stream that hears,
> The flowing of all men's tears beneath the sky.

Whistler was buried in Chiswick cemetery beside his
wife, and near to Hogarth. In the churchyard policemen
were drawn up to restrain the expected crowd. But no
crowd came. Whistler died more quietly than he had
lived, and the restless spirit which had traveled so far, from
Lowell to St. Petersburg and from Washington to Paris,
rested at last upon the banks of the river which had become a part of himself, and the beauty of which he had
portrayed better than any other artist. The art which he
had learned in Paris he used to picture London, and he

gave to its inhabitants new eyes with which to regard their own city. An Englishman he never became and would have scorned to be thought, but he gained something from his long residence in England and gave much in return. London was peculiarly his own city. He did not leave it gladly.

Whistler loved life with a feverish intensity. There was in his entire composition no trace of that Timon of Athens attitude, which characterized Degas in his later years. He loved society, loved even its frivolity so long as it had elegance also, and upper-class London provided just what his nature craved—a background and an audience for the display of his personality. He was not Timon, he was Cyrano, tilting at the Academies, refusing to conform to accepted standards, *gentilhomme* in a rather old-fashioned sense. He never accepted the English notions of gentlemanly behavior.

To be quietly dressed, to be inconspicuous, to conceal one's real feelings, to be a member of a caste rather than an individual, never appealed to him. His plume flowed the braver because all his fellows had cut such conspicuous appendages from their head-gear. He was the born duelist. For consequences he cared nothing, for causes only incidentally; it was enough for him that he could return from the conflict with a dozen abandoned hats impaled on his rapier.

Yet, like Cyrano, he had a fundamental seriousness of

purpose. He vindicated the individual against conformity and he defended the artist against the Philistine. And this he could do far more sincerely than the esthete, for that typical product of the English upper middle classes was only too often what Whistler called Wilde—bourgeois in spite of himself. It is easy to find his gestures extravagant, his scorn excessive, his attacks ill-directed, his touchy sense of honor a trifle ridiculous. These things must necessarily be when the soul of a seventeenth-century free-liver is reborn in the body of a nineteenth-century artist. He loved good living, the elegancies of life were a necessity to him, yet he more than once flung away his fortune for a punctilio. What madness, yet what a gesture!

The strange little man, half charlatan, half dancing master as he seemed to his contemporaries, is, in the end, a noble figure. He fought the good fight however much it was entwined with his own personal animosities, he kept the faith however much it was entangled with his own conceit.

Soon after his death, his friends, and especially those who were members of the International Society of Sculptors, Painters and Gravers, set a movement on foot for the erection of a memorial. It was proposed to set up a figure of a winged victory in the gardens stretching along Chelsea Embankment, and Rodin, the new president of the International Society, was asked if he would undertake the work. He consented very readily and because of his friendship for Whistler declared that he would charge only for the casting of the statue and not for his own work. The sum required was about two thousand pounds, and the London County Council agreed to give the land on which the statue was to rest.

Whistler had always been unfortunate with his subscription lists. The plain man gives his money to the champion of righteous causes, but Whistler had never seemed to him to be a champion of anything but his own notoriety. In this the plain man was wrong, but the effect was the same as if he had been right, and Whistler during his lifetime appealed to the public in vain. The appeal, of course, was half ironical, for he expected nothing.

The Memorial Fund was more successful, yet subscriptions came in very slowly, and at the end of two years had not yet amounted to the sum required. However, public interest was gradually aroused, and the energy of Pennell and Heinemann raised the fund to the required level.[2] The money was in hand. It remained but for Rodin to produce the work. He wrote in 1908 that it needed only a few months more. In 1909 he wired: "The Whistler monu-

[2] Pennell's extraordinary prejudice in anything concerning Whistler is nowhere more glaringly shown than in his account of this subscription list. (See "The Whistler Journal" [Philadelphia, 1921], p. 302). "Henry James, Thomas Hardy, Maurice Hewlett, Austin Dobson, Rudyard Kipling, Bernard Shaw, H. G. Wells, Edmund Gosse, and George Trevelyan were glad to honor the memory of a man for whom they had done little during his lifetime." They should have left their own work to do something for Whistler! Why should they? And what could they have done?

ment is the preoccupation of my every day." In 1913: "The Whistler monument is approaching completion." In 1916, Rodin was promising to deliver it within six months after the end of the war.

When Rodin died, the committee appointed to administer the fund went to Paris to inspect the unfinished monument. They rejected it, and the money, at long last, was returned to the subscribers. Perhaps if St. Gaudens had been asked instead of Rodin, as Frederick MacMonnies suggested, Whistler might have had his memorial and Chelsea another statue. What does it matter? The river itself commemorates him every time that the blue dusk creeps along its banks. It is better that he should remain impalpable, impersonal, he who while he lived was continually diverting attention from his painting to his own person.

His death called forth such a flood of personal reminiscences that his art was for the moment lost sight of, yet it was obviously necessary to "place" Whistler in the history of nineteenth-century art, and those who had criticized his work while he lived made preparations for their final verdict.

Whistler had always treated Wedmore when they met with the contempt which he reserved for the professional critic. He made a point of spiking his anecdotes at dinner parties, of pricking the bubble of what he regarded as his self-importance. Wedmore was singularly forgiving. He really admired Whistler and made an early catalogue of his etchings. When Whistler died he wrote an article in a review in which he endeavored to sum up the whole matter. "Was it," he asked in his own highly mannered fashion, "a master who had brought a revelation, and who held the key to all truths; a greater painter than Velasquez, the peer, more than the peer of Rembrandt? Or was it a mannerist, smart, brilliant, versed in the jugglery of *chic* —a painter and etcher sworn to eccentricity: and whom only the genuineness of his shallow opinions saved from the disgrace of a charlatan?"

Certainly "versed in the jugglery of *chic*" is an excellent phrase to describe one aspect of Whistler's art, but the rest of Wedmore's article consists of a description of Whistler's work in etching and lithography, and he offers no complete answer to the question posed in his opening paragraph.

The issue was more solidly faced by Roger Fry.[3] Whistler was the hierophant of the religion of beauty and in the face of a mocking and sentimental world he proclaimed the gallant but entirely erroneous doctrine that beauty is self-contained. The result of this theory was unfortunate for his own art. Could his mordant wit have been translated into terms of satire, could he have faced life instead of shrinking from it, he might have created

[3] "Watts and Whistler," by Roger E. Fry, Quarterly Review, No. 103, April 1905, p. 607.

something vital, passionate, immortal. His fastidiousness was his own worst enemy. The great artist is almost always a gross feeder, in the sense that he does not need to arrange the menu before he sits down to the meal. Whistler "almost sank the genius in the man of taste." Indeed his most valuable legacy to European painting was probably his enthusiasm for the Japanese and his feat of educating the western public to an appreciation of the Japanese angle of vision. "Certain it is that what was most original in Whistler's art was in part due to his power, not as a creator, but as a connoisseur. He discovered, not Battersea Bridge, but the Bridge of Kyoto; and Hiroshige rather than nature taught him the perfect harmonies of the nocturnes. But taste, which thus led him to refine on life and reject its invitations, however chaste, is like asceticism, a negative and cloistered virtue." The writer even speaks of Whistler's artistic Calvinism. "Whistler accomplished something which had never been done before, accomplished it finally and definitively. It is something palpable and evident, but it scarcely claims the very highest rank."

The first frontal attack on Whistler's reputation came from the German critic, Julius Meier-Graefe, whose monumental work on modern art was translated into English in 1908.[4] His opinion of English art altogether was extremely unflattering, and he insisted on regarding Whistler as pri-

[4] "Modern Art," by Julius Meier-Graefe, from the German by Florence Simonds and George W. Chrystal (London, 1908).

marily an English artist. He was "fundamentally an
unfrocked Pre-Raphaelite," and Pre-Raphaelitism itself
was a "criminal conspiracy" that tore up by the roots all
the centenarian elements of a native art capable of development. "The hundred skins in which nature and his
own dexterity in disguises enveloped him conceal a perfectly English core." Yet everything that happened in
European art during the mid-nineteenth century was re-
flected in his own work. He was aware of developments in
Paris, and it was this cosmopolitanism of his—in itself a
weakness—which gave him his enormous reputation. To
the English he stood against a background of European
culture of which they were only dimly aware. To the
French he was almost the only artist working in England,
and was therefore magnified against a background of what
they regarded as complete barbarism.

Even Meier-Graefe's praise of Whistler is a little back-
handed. He speaks of the brilliant pattern of "At the
Piano," the "Carlyle" and the "Mother," the dexterity with
which the profile is set against the wall, the distinction of
the pose, and goes on to say that these canvases have all the
qualities of the true Salon picture. "Indulgent critics of
the future will no doubt bracket Whistler with Fantin.
They were very similar powers of a totally different kind.
Both stand aloof from the great artistic achievements of the
nineteenth century, the one deliberately, the other involun-
tarily. Neither was a creator in the true sense, both trans-

[ 298 ]

formed inherited materials, and the results of their activity were not indispensable to modern art-development."

The protest which can be entered here is that it is possible to be an important artist without necessarily diverting the stream of art. The professional art historian inevitably tends to think influences more important than achievements, or rather he falls into the habit of considering them to be almost the same thing.

With the literary appreciation of the late nineteenth-century Frenchmen, Meier-Graefe will have nothing to do. Where, in the "White Girl," they saw the evocation of a spirit, he sees nothing but "glass eyes, false hair, clothes, carpet, and curtains." In plain terms, "there are no spirits, and nothing happens of itself, least of all in art, which knows nothing of the arbitrary and accidental."

Even the nocturnes fare hardly at the German critic's hands. They are not without charm, and many of them show a highly cultivated taste. No educated person can now walk along the bank of the Thames at nightfall without thinking of Whistler. Yet Whistler chose Nature in her weaker manifestations in order to conquer her more easily. "He chose her so small that nothing remains of her but a nebulous veil."

Yet even Meier-Graefe admits the beauty of the "Miss Alexander," and of many of the water-colors, etchings, and lithographs, and concludes that he was a "little master," an industrial artist of delicate taste, a stimulating

[ 299 ]

influence which we may turn to good account. It would
have been nothing less than miraculous if America, as yet
without artistic traditions, had contrived to bring forth a
great artist. Hence Whistler's insistence on the isolation of
the artist, in order to justify his own existence.

The same point is made by the English critic, Charles
Marriott.[5] "Whistler stood for that impossible thing, a cosmopolitan art. . . . It is art divorced from life and depend-
ing entirely upon culture. . . . Whistler was a fine artist,
but his philosophy of art was not only unsound, but un-
easy. Otherwise he would not have needed to talk and write
so much about it. . . . The truth is, that, with all its peculiar charm, the art of Whistler was based upon a series
of compromises and evasions. The French Impressionists
pursued the theory of Realism to its logical conclusion . . .
[Whistler's] larger works, at any rate, are efforts to escape
from the logic of Realism into a region of twilight and
undertones. Lacking the imagination, or perhaps the courage, to translate the facts of nature boldly into terms of his
medium, he waited for or invented conditions in which
the facts would not be too obvious, and made them 'decorative' by arrangements that were entirely lacking in the
logic of design."

Certain modern American critics also—feeling no
doubt that there was an element of Chauvinism in Pennell's exaggeration of the accomplishment of Whistler—

[5] "Modern Movements in Painting," by C. Marriott (London, 1920).

have tended to be more severe in their estimate than their colleagues in England, although none of them has pushed denigration so far as Meier-Graefe.

One of the most recent, Frank Jewett Mather,[6] includes him among the "twilight" impressionists like Carrière and Cazin, and concludes: "Whistler's fastidiously reticent art, a thing of whispers and raised eyelids, is charming, just that and nothing more. . . . His lucidity and satire was useful in riddling a galvanized official art, but he had no better esthetic than the faith that art will happen. . . . He did a rather small thing amazingly well, and in retrospect I fear his delightful art will diminish. It hung too much on his wit and personal legend. He had the magnificent background of Victorian London and the Royal Academy. His exotic brilliance too easily dominated such a scene."

Whistler's reputation is suffering from an inevitable reaction, and perhaps will never stand quite so high as it did thirty years ago. He pays the penalty of impressing himself too vigorously on the world, for it is not those who inspire the most fanatical personal discipleship who always found a school to revere their names when they are dead, and carry their principles into practice. What Whistler said is even yet of interest to apprentice wits. But is what Whistler painted of interest to budding artists?

The dominant influences which still control painting

[6] "Modern Painting," by Frank Jewett Mather (New York, 1927).

in England derive, like Whistler's own art, from France; but they only flowed indirectly through him. The New English Art Club, which Whistler thought so wholly ridiculous, received and transmitted the lessons of Manet, Monet, and Degas. The first exhibition was held at the Marlborough Gallery, Pall Mall, in 1886. Steer and Professor Brown were among the original members, and Sickert appeared in their midst two years later. Sickert, as we have seen, was at one time Whistler's most ardent disciple, and he retained a modified Whistlerianism for some years. It is therefore only in a minor degree and almost by accident that Whistler has part in the movement which was to revolutionize English painting. He was, indeed, patron of the school [7] which Sickert and Alfred Thornton opened in De Morgan's old studio in the Vale (that same cul-de-sac which had witnessed the furious altercation between the not-yet-discarded Maud and the future Mrs. Whistler); but the school was a failure, and in any case influence by teaching can be gained only by long devotion, such as that which Legros gave to the Slade. The part played by the Slade in the development of modern painting should not be forgotten, although it has been overlaid by more startling influences, but with that, too, Whistler had nothing to do.

Whistler was a superb decorator, and his influence on

[7] "Walter Richard Sickert," by Alfred Thornton. Artwork, Vol. VI, No. 21, p. 1.

decoration continues. If we no longer load our rooms with knickknacks, if we prefer our walls plainly distempered, if we hang few pictures instead of many, and prefer Chinese matting to rose-embroidered carpets, it is at least as much his doing as anyone else's. But in painting it is another story. He was too personal and too sophisticated. The neo-primitives of the modern studios, the admirers of Negro art, the "strong" painters of today can have little use for an artist whose canvases were the epitome of all that is refined, civilized, and reticent. The later impressionists with their "treble" palet are the complete antitheses of Whistlerian twilight, and it is from them that modern painting derives its color. The disciples of Cézanne, the apostles of "construction in depth," attempt the very opposite of Whistler's careful flattening, his narrowing of planes; and it is from them and from the exponents of the geometrical that modern painters derive their interest in form.

So far as modern easel-painting is concerned, Whistler is in complete eclipse, was so, indeed, before he died. Yet the elimination of the anecdote which has liberated painting from the trammels of literature and left it free to develop in accordance with the laws of its own nature was, partly at least, his work, and for that we may be grateful, and for that he may still be honored. The name of "greatest painter of the nineteenth century," which his first biographers so rashly bestowed upon him, may be disputed by

many artists—by Constable, by Ingres, by Manet, by Degas
—but his own particular niche is secure. What he set out
to do, he did with singular perfection, and that is all we
have the right to demand of any artist.


## The End

# BIBLIOGRAPHICAL NOTE

A N adequate Whistler bibliography is entirely outside the scope of the present volume; it would need a volume to itself. His habit of bringing out a little pamphlet after every quarrel, the upheaval which attended the publication of "The Gentle Art of Making Enemies," the foreign translations of his "Ten o'Clock," his annotated catologues, and the rest would swell even a summary bibliography to unwieldy proportions.

To keep track of the comment and criticism he evoked is an even more formidable task. For the greater part of his active life and for years after his death, Whistler was *news*. Not only his art but his personality was caricatured and ridiculed; and he knew so many people in his active social existence that the crop of reminiscences and recollections which appeared after his death was unusually large.

I will therefore confine myself to indicating, by way of acknowledgment, those publications which I have found most useful. First of course must come the "Life" (1908) by Joseph and Elizabeth Robins Pennell, supplemented by the "Journal" (1921) which is even more interesting and instructive. Théodore Duret's book ("Histoire de J. A. M.

[ 305 ]

Whistler et Son Œuvre," 1904) must not be forgotten. It is an admirably sane and balanced account, a tribute of friendship refreshingly free from partizan bias. Mortimer Menpes's "Whistler as I Knew Him" (1905) is amusing, and full of sidelights on Whistler's character by a disciple who kept his liking for Whistler although he lost his friendship. For the period immediately following the Ruskin trial, O. H. Bacher's "With Whistler in Venice" (1908) is invaluable, and there are stories of Venice in an article by W. Scott, published in the Studio (1904, p. 97). Oswald Sickert and G. H. Boughton, R. A., contributed to the same volume. A special "Whistler Portfolio" was issued by the Studio in 1905. W. M. Chase wrote an article in the Century Magazine (LXXV, 1908, p. 928) in which he described "The Two Whistlers: Recollections of a Summer with the Great Etcher."

Whistler's attempt to found or direct a school is dealt with in C. Cuneo's "Whistler's Academy of Painting" in the Century Magazine (LXXIII, 1906, p. 19); while M. A. Mullikin contributed his "Reminiscences of the Whistler Academy" to the Studio (XXXIV, 1905, p. 237). Whistler's relations with Frederick Keppel are amusingly set forth in his "One Day with Whistler" (1911). D. C. Seitz brought out a volume of "Whistler Stories" (1913). Thomas R. Way's "Memories of James McNeill Whistler" is an admirable account of the master with especial reference to his work in lithography. Malcolm C. Salaman was one of the earliest champions of Whistler and contributed to the Court and Society Review (July 1, 1886) a valuable description of the Fulham Road Studio.

Almost any volume of English reminiscences covering the last thirty years of the nineteenth century contains some mention of Whistler. The most valuable is the "Memoir of Thomas Armstrong, C. B." (1912), for Armstrong was a fellow student in Paris and devotes the greater part of his book to reminiscences of Whistler and Du Maurier. Our knowledge of his student days and of the early years in London is almost entirely derived from Armstrong and from the letters of Whistler to Fantin quoted by Léonce Bénédite in the Gazette des Beaux Arts (XXXIII, XXXIV, 1905). W. M. Rossetti's diary (1903) describes the period when Whistler was collecting Blue China and Japanese prints, and his "Dante Gabriel Rossetti, Family Letters with a Memoir" (1895) may also be consulted. G. P. Jacomb-Hood's "With Brush and Pencil" (1925) gives a good description of the intrigues which led to Whistler's election as president of the Society of British Artists, while the Grosvenor Gallery period is well handled in "Naphtali" by C. Lewis Hind (1926). Light is thrown on Whistler's relations with Sir Coutts and Lady Lindsay and with the Godwins in Mrs. Jopling-Rowe's "Twenty Years of My Life" (1925). "An Artist's Life in London and Paris" by A. Ludovici (1926) contains a great deal of valuable information about Whistler by one who knew him intimately for many years. Mention should also be made of Dr. G. C. Williamson's "Murray Marks and His Friends" (1919). Arthur Symons's vivid personal impressions are to be found in the volume of studies which he called "From Toulouse-Lautrec to Rodin" (1929).

Of foreign criticism and reminiscence there is no lack. Duret has been mentioned already, but a study by H. W. Singer appeared in 1904, and in the following year Camille Mauclair's "De Watteau à Whistler." J. K. Huysmans devotes a chapter to Whistler in "Certains" (1908) and Jacques Émile Blanche, in "De David à Degas" (1919), gives a most valuable account of Whistler's technique.

Notes for a Whistler bibliography were collected by T. R. Way and published in the Book-Lovers' Magazine (VI, 1905, p. 14). A more complete list is given by D. C. Seitz in his "Writings by and about James Abbott McNeill Whistler" (1910), and there is a "Catalogue of Works by J. A. McN. Whistler, with a Bibliography" (4th edition, 1921) issued by the Victoria and Albert Museum. An "Iconography of Portraits and Caricatures of J. McN. Whistler" was compiled by A. E. Gallatin and published in 1913.

INDEX

# INDEX

INDEX

[ 314 ]

INDEX

"White Girl, The," 79, 103, 104, 106, 109, 125, 126, 168, 260, 264, 299

Wilde, Oscar, 212-15, 220, 230, 293

Williams, Captain, 51

Williamson, Dr. G. C., 196, 308

Winans, Ross, 30

Wren, Sir Christopher, 100

Zola, Emile, 44, 60, 70, 114, 116, 246